SPINNING DESIGNER YARNS

Diane Varney, 1952-

INTERWEAVE PRESS
306 North Washington Avenue
Loveland, Colorado 80537

Illustrations by Ann Sabin
Photography by Joe Coca
Typesetting by Marc M. Owens
Cover by Signorella Graphic Arts

 INTERWEAVE PRESS
306 North Washington Avenue
Loveland, Colorado 80537

Contents

Introduction

I assume you know how to spin, at least a little, and want to be more creative with your yarns and have more fun with your spinning. This is a book of ideas and encouragement. Handspun yarns can be white and lumpy, or they can be gray and precise — or they can be as colorful and deliciously textured as your imagination.

When I design and execute a project using handspun yarn, I want to like it right away when it is new and I want to like it for a long time. I want my finished projects to become dear friends. I have found that the difference between a project I hate and one I love is often in the amount of design work which went into it: time spent designing is well spent.

My concept of designer yarn is of yarn spun with a clear concept of the effect I want to create. It is unique and interesting yarn, well thought out and well crafted, that cannot be found coming from the spinning mills.

We spinners have so much potential, and so much power: we can create the perfect yarn for a project we have in mind. We don't have to rely on the spinning mills. We can make the yarn we want. I believe that we often underestimate our abilities and our potential and make whatever yarn the wheel churns out; I know I did that for a long time.

As one indication of how much more could be done in the area of yarn design than has been, we don't even have a common group of words to describe special yarns. The names used for different yarns are often conflicting and confusing. The same yarn structure will have three names in three different sources. I have tried here to use the names most commonly found for particular yarns and to give alternates where possible. In some cases I have had to make up names.

Let's not design by default, let's design through choice. Let's make informed, intelligent decisions about the yarn we make. And let's have more fun spinning. My primary goal in writing this book is to inspire you. I'd like it to help you explore new techniques, plan more, and strive for wider horizons.

I believe that project design must come first, before yarn design. I'd rather know where I'm going than spin lots of yarn and then try to come up with a way to use it. The problem with the "yarn first" approach is that the yarn is never just right for any project. There's always some way in which it could have been better. If only there had been a bit more twist, or the yarn had been a little thinner. . . . And then there's never *enough* yarn. Who says spinning is relaxing? Sometimes simply using up all that handspun becomes a goal, instead of creating something wonderful and unique with it.

While this "design first" approach implies a lot of conscious decisions, it must be built on a foundation of experience. Where do you get that experience, the ideas, the sense of which aspect of a yarn to change so it will be perfect? Through playing!

So at the same time that I'm urging you to control your yarn I'll be helping you loosen up and explore. These two approaches aren't opposites — they are partners.

May you find food for thought and action here, and may all your projects bring you joy from their first moments.

GENERAL CONSIDERATIONS

Spinning wheels

Your spinning wheel will determine to some extent the types of yarns you can spin, although most spinners should be able to spin all of the types of yarn in this book on whatever wheel they have. We are all looking for the perfect wheel, which will spin all weights and types of yarn. Well, it doesn't exist, although some wheels offer more flexibility than others. It follows that some wheels are better at spinning one kind of yarn than another.

The limiting factors of spinning wheels

The potentially limiting factors include the ratio of the wheel (a measure of the speed at which it operates), the capacity of the bobbin, the size of the orifice, and the size of the hooks on the flyer. If your wheel is limited in one of these respects, you may have to compensate.

A wheel's ratio is determined by comparing the size of the driving wheel to the part which it drives, which will be a pulley on either the bobbin or flyer. You don't need to know precisely what your wheel's ratio is in order to be able to design and control yarns, but a working knowledge of how ratio affects that wheel's spinning capacity and an awareness

Fast wheels and slow wheels

of whether your wheel is slow, medium, or fast will help you understand how to do what you want. A fast wheel, with a ratio of, for example, 20:1, will insert more twists for each movement of the treadle than will a slow wheel, with a ratio of, say, 3:1. It will also insert more twists before drawing the yarn onto the bobbin.

It is easier to spin fine yarns on a fast (high-ratio) wheel and bulky, low-twist yarns on a slow (low-ratio) wheel. Some so-called "production" wheels have 18:1 or 20:1 ratios; bulk or Indian spinners have low ratios, like 2:1 or 3:1. Most "antique" wheels were designed to spin fine yarns, and have relatively high ratios. Many of the commonly available modern wheels have two pulley positions. The larger diameter pulley causes the wheel to spin at a ratio of about 7:1; the smaller diameter pulley speeds it up to somewhere around 12:1. You can choose which of these ratios best suits your dexterity or a specific project.

Some of the techniques covered in this book require a fair amount of coordination and hand movement. It may be easier to learn these techniques on a low-ratio wheel or setting, since you'll have more time — relative to the rate of twist insertion — to move your hands around.

Size of orifice

A wheel's orifice must be large enough to accommodate the yarn which must pass through it. Most orifices on modern wheels measure between $3/8$ to $5/8$ inch. Some wheels come with adapters which can be inserted in the basic hole to reduce the size of the orifice. An orifice which is larger than your yarn would not seem to be a problem, but sometimes the rotation of the flyer will make the yarn jerk in a large orifice at each revolution, which can make you put bumps in your yarn where you don't want them. A few wheels have no orifice; instead, they have an extra hook at the front of the flyer through which the yarn feeds. These wheels can handle some heavily textured yarns that other wheels won't accept.

Flyer hooks

The hooks on the flyer must also allow your yarn to pass onto the bobbin. Textured yarns may catch or snag on small hooks. If this happens repeatedly, you may become frustrated. You can avoid this by spinning finer yarns or by making less textured versions of offending types of yarns.

Adjust your wheel, or modify the yarn

If you are having trouble spinning a particular yarn on your wheel, try adjusting the speed of your treadling (usually you need to go more slowly on a high-ratio wheel, or more quickly on a low-ratio one) or the tension on the drive and/or brake bands. You can also modify the yarn design slightly so it will flow more smoothly.

Sampling

I am a fervent believer in sampling. Yes, it takes extra time, but it is time well spent. After I started to sample, I liked almost all my finished projects. The opposite was true before.

I believe that designing works best when you can select the most appropriate yarn from several possibilities. When you have an idea of the kind of yarn you think will be suitable for a project, spin some. Then spin at least two similar yarns, but change some aspect of the yarn's design. Add more twist, try a slightly thicker yarn, or add some flecks of colored fiber. Keep trying variations until you are satisfied.

Spin several samples

Make a fabric swatch

Once you have selected what you think will be the best yarn, make a fabric sample by knitting, weaving, or crocheting it. Determine your sett or stitch gauge and shrinkage. Do you like the fabric? Is it the best way to use the yarn? Is it the right weight? Does it drape appropriately? Is there any way to improve it?

To be able to spin consistent yarn for a project, you must record all the necessary information about how you produced it. Keep track of the fiber and its preparation, the number of twists per inch, the yards per pound of the resulting yarn, and which wheel or ratio adjustment you used if you have options. Did you wash the yarn after spinning? Did you dry it on a yarn blocker or simply hang it up? These factors all make a difference.

Record the necessary information

Each sample will give you information that you can use not only for the project at hand but for future projects. Keep your samples and organize them. The best method I have found for filing samples requires a notebook — I like 8½ by 11 inches — filled with posterboard pages, which are firm enough to hold yarn samples and still lie flat. If you buy the posterboard at an artists' supply store you can probably get it cut to size. Wrap your yarn samples around the posterboard sheets so that you have four or five wraps and tie the ends together in the back. Just below each yarn sample, record all the pertinent information. If you outgrow your three-ring binder you can use a small file-folder case with a handle.

Keep and organize your samples

I also like to collect samples of interesting commercial yarns. I keep these in my notebook with my handspun samples. Good samples are the foundation upon which good work is built.

Finishing yarn

Almost all yarns benefit from having the twist set. Setting makes the yarns easier to work with, and they become less likely to curl and kink up as you work with them. Setting or not setting the twist can also affect the shape and hand of your finished project.

Set the twist

I skein the yarn directly from the bobbin, then wash it gently to remove the last traces of dye and dirt. It is a light and gentle washing. Some spinners like to add a little creme rinse of fabric softener to the final rinse water to soften their yarn. I generally use the spin cycle of my washing machine to remove any excess water and then I hang the skeins to dry.

All of the yarn for a given project should receive the same finishing treatment. I once wove a beautiful throw with all handspun yarns. The weft was a gray singles, and there was one little skein I hadn't washed; the rest of the weft had been washed and hung in skeins to dry. I wove approximately two inches with that unfinished skein. After I washed the completed throw I discovered that the two-inch section had shrunk so my edges had big indentations at that point.

A yarn blocker is handy for finishing yarn. Wind the yarn directly from the bobbin to the blocker, and then steam it with a small clothing steamer or immerse the entire blocker cage in water to moisten the yarn. The greater the tension under which you wind the yarn onto the blocker, the less elasticity you will have in your finished yarn. Skeins which have been set on a yarn blocker have a much more professional appearance; anyone who plans to sell yarn should consider using one.

Occasionally a more severe finishing treatment may be in order. Garnetted yarns — those with small bits of contrasting fiber spun in — often have nubs that are not completely secured into the yarn. A shock treatment, such as boiling briefly and then rinsing with cold water, will felt the yarn slightly and make the nubs more secure.

Some yarns may need more shocking treatment

Commercial yarns

Like most people, my time is limited and valuable. I could spin all of the yarns I use in my handspun projects, but I can't see much reason to do so if I can get the effect I want with commercial yarns. I primarily use commercial yarns for cores and binders in fancy plied yarns. I used to believe that using commercial yarns was somehow less pure, but I have decided now that it is just plain sensible. My goal is to make beautiful yarns and then wonderful things with those yarns. I often buy fine yarns with the sole intent of incorporating them into my handspun yarns.

THINKING ABOUT DESIGN

Design has been described as simply *planning ahead*. To begin the design process, you need to make some basic decisions about the project, because these decisions will influence your later yarn decisions.

Designing the project

What item do you want to make? Some possibilities include a blanket, sweater, rug, towel, upholstery fabric, tablecloth, belt, shirt, skirt, poncho. Each of these requires different yarn characteristics.

How will it be used? Think of its location, its purpose, and the projected amount of wear which it will have to withstand. If the project is a rug, will it be used by the front door, next to your bed, or hung on the wall? If it is a sweater, will you wear it to the barn to milk the goats, or to work at the office, or to the symphony in the winter?

How do you want it to look? You need to think of color, texture, and weight. If the project is a pair of mittens, will they be medium-weight, multicolored, and superfuzzy, or heavy, one-color, and knitted with a pattern stitch? If the project is a sweater, should it have an intricate Fair Isle pattern, or do you want to emphasize an exciting textured yarn, perhaps a bouclé?

How durable should it be? You will need to decide if you are making a relatively temporary stylish accent or an heirloom. If the project is a garment, is it more important for it to follow current fashion and last for three or four years, or do you want to wear it every day for twenty years and still have it look good enough for your grandchild to wear it for another twenty?

What structure will be used? Knitting, crochet, weaving, and other techniques all make specific demands on yarns.

Is warmth important? For a garment or blanket, your climate may have some requirements.

How will it be cleaned?

As you work through these questions, others will occur to you. The more answers you have in advance the better you will be able to produce the work you have in mind.

Think about what you want to make

Yarn design

Once you have designed the project, you can consider the yarns. Yarn design involves all of the characteristics which could describe a yarn, like:

thickness	amount of plying twist
amount of twist	loft
direction of twist	softness
fiber type	uniformity
fiber color	color/pattern interactions
texture	spacing of design elements
luster	susceptibility to pilling
single strand or plied	expected durability
number of plies	expected appearance of
plying direction	yarn after some wear.

Think about the type of yarn you need

Thickness, loft, and spinning method

Decisions about each of these factors become easy when you know what your project will be. A very basic decision concerns *yarn thickness and loft*. This choice is influenced by the thickness, weight, and feel you want in your finished fabric, by the method you'll use to make the fabric (weaving, knitting, etc.), and by whether you will ply the yarn. Lightweight fine fabrics come from finer, thinner yarns. I'll never forget my first handspun sweater. It was a cardigan that wasn't especially large, but it weighed at least four pounds. I knitted it with heavy yarn on small needles, and it may have been bulletproof. It was not a dear friend to me.

You can't get a thin fabric from a thick yarn

Another choice is whether to make a *worsted or woolen* type of yarn. Two yarns can appear to be the same thickness, yet the weight and handling characteristics of each can be quite different, depending on how it was spun. Basically, worsted yarns are extremely strong, smooth durable yarns. They are spun from relatively parallel fibers. Woolen yarns, on the other hand, are made from randomly oriented fibers and they are soft, warmer (because they incorporate more insulating air space), and not as hard-wearing as worsteds.

Your choice of fleece may determine which of these two preparation and spinning techniques you will use; a fine, short, crimpy Merino would make a grand woolen-spun yarn but a lousy worsted, while a coarse, long, shiny, and low-crimp Lincoln asks to be worsted and resists woolen. Preparation for worsted spinning includes washing and combing techniques that preserve the parallel fiber arrangement found in the original locks and remove all shorter fibers. Fleece for woolen spinning is picked and then carded, to create even fiber density for smooth spinning while obliterating the original parallel alignment.

The differences between worsted and woolen can be summarized as follows:

	Worsted	Woolen
Fiber arrangement	Highly parallel	More random
Fiber length	Longer, all fibers equal	Long and short
Ability to insulate	Lower (cool)	Higher (warm)
Strength	Stronger	Weaker
Weight	Heavier	Lighter
Luster	Enhanced	Diminished

To ply or not to ply

Since plied yarns take more than twice as long to spin as singles, I like to have a good reason to ply. The decision of whether to ply or not is affected by how durable the yarn needs to be, the weight of the finished fabric, and the fiber structure (for example, the knitting stitch or woven pattern) the design calls for.

Plying can increase a yarn's strength

Plied yarns are stronger than singles. If one strand of a two-ply yarn is broken, the other will keep a hole from forming in the fabric. Plying is the only way to get a structurally sound thick yarn from short-staple fibers.

Plying also adds loft to a yarn. A two-ply is not as heavy as a singles of the same thickness, and that added loft can produce a garment that is warmer, lighter in weight, and more comfortable than a similar garment made from a singles yarn.

It's simple to achieve interesting special effects by plying yarns of different fibers together, such as shiny silk with a heathered wool blend.

If you want to emphasize a fiber's luster, you will want to ply. The process makes the individual strands appear to lie more parallel to the strand of yarn.

Singles slant

The subject of plying brings up the issue of the dreaded *singles slant*. If you knit an unset or overtwisted *singles* yarn into stockinette stitch, the unbalanced twist causes the fabric to slant. A knitted square loses its right angles and leans seriously to one side. Sometimes this malady doesn't show up until you wash the completed fabric. Blocking will not reverse the problem. Once I knitted a beautiful vest of fine singles wool with cables up the front. After washing, the whole thing slanted, cables and all. The moral of this story is: always take your sample swatches all the way through the washing process.

Slanting is most evident in stockinette. But there is a trick that can help you out of a bind. If you knit into the *back* of each knit stitch instead of into the front, the slanting will be eliminated. This "pseudo-stockinette" is similar, but not identical, to normal stockinette.

There are many other knitting stitches where singles slant is not a problem. Lower-twist yarns also have less of a tendency to slant than high-twist yarns. Proper sampling should reveal both difficult situations and some solutions. Plying usually eliminates this troublesome habit.

Durability

Commercial sweater designers and manufacturers seem to have little regard for the durability of their garments. You can often see snagged yarns when clothes are still on store racks. Fashionability comes first, reliability last.

At the opposite end of things, there is a school of spinning thought that equates quality with durability. I believe that durability is one important component of quality. However, as a spinner with the ability to *choose* and to *design*, you will find that sometimes you can't have it all. You won't be able to make a light, fluffy, soft sweater which will stand up to 30 years of hard wear. It just won't work. You'll need to decide which attributes of "quality" are most important to you. But if you know which factors are *your* top priorities, you will be able to maximize the important qualities and minimize the undesirable ones.

Decide what "quality" means to you

In general, textured yarns are not as durable as smooth yarns, because the textured elements often project from the finished fabric and are subject to additional wear. They are also often not firmly twisted, which is part of their charm.

The principles here apply not only to yarn but to the way we use it. The "bobbles" knitted into a garment will have to endure more wear than the surrounding stockinette areas.

As spinners, we can strengthen the abrasion-prone parts of our yarns and garments. We can strengthen certain parts of our projects by using stronger fibers, plied yarns, or the techniques of worsted spinning. We can make specific yarns thicker, more compact, or more highly twisted.

Yarn Durability		
	More durable	Less durable
Fiber length	Longer	Shorter
Yarn type	Worsted	Woolen
Texture	Less	More
Twist	More	Less
Plying	Plied yarn	Singles
Fiber diameter	Larger	Smaller

Pilling

Pilling—the fuzzing up of those little nubs of fiber on a finished garment, usually between the sleeves and body or around the bottom ribbing—is an aesthetic problem, not a structural one. Pills start when shorter fibers come to the surface of a fabric and are rubbed into little, semi-felted clumps on the surface.

Nobody likes pills, although they don't weaken the fabric. If you're capable of ignoring them, you can do so. Or maybe you'll take a few minutes now and then to pick them off, as Elizabeth Zimmermann suggests. If you detest them sufficiently, you can go to great lengths of extra fiber preparation and spin only special pill-resistant types of yarn, which may or may not keep them satisfactorily at bay. You can minimize pilling by using long-staple fibers, combing them, and spinning them with the worsted techniques. Shearing pills off with electric clippers is not recommended; you can too easily slit the fabric in the process.

Interactions between color, texture, and fabric structure

When you make a project, you work with both the design of the yarn and the design of the structure it becomes part of: the knitting stitch, the weave structure, the basketry technique. Predicting the interaction between yarn design and fabric structure is a skill that comes with practice, but there are some general principles that will help you forecast your results.

The eye is drawn to contrast

The eye is drawn to the strongest contrast in a piece. Contrast can occur in the yarn or in the fabric, and if you use it casually you may find various types of contrast having a fight for dominance. For example, you knit a sweater with a chevron stitch, using all space-dyed yarn. The yarn includes both light and dark colors. When you finish, you discover that the light and dark areas of the yarn command much more attention than the carefully knitted zigzags of your chevrons, and the sweater's impact is muddled.

Fancy yarns are often most effective as accents, used to contrast with adjacent plain yarns. It doesn't take much of a fancy yarn to dress up a fabric. If you want to use a lot of fancy yarn, it will show up best in a simple structure, such as plain weave or stockinette.

A textured yarn will obscure the texture inherent in a fabric's structure or pattern. The more textured the yarn, the less obvious your pattern will be. For example, a cabled sweater knit with a bouclé or a fuzzy angora will not have crisp, distinct cables. The same is true in weaving: complicated patterns are more visible when worked in smooth yarns.

Light-colored yarns tend to show off fabric structures better than dark-colored yarns. If you have seen an Aran sweater made with a dark yarn, you will know what I mean. The shadows in a light-colored fabric throw the knitted pattern into relief.

Thick elements (such as slubs or knots) tend to stay on the purl side of a knitted fabric, since as the fabric is made the yarn is pulled through loops. The thicker parts are too fat to make it to the front side. If a textured yarn is the focus of your knitting project, you may want to avoid large quantities of stockinette. You can emphasize the yarn's irregularities by planning to use the reverse stockinette (purl) side as the finished side. Or you could work garter stitch, which results in a finished side composed of 50 percent purl stitches. Or you could pay attention and pull the lumps through to the front side of the stockinette areas.

Fancy or textured yarns work best in simple structures

Light-colored yarns show off intricate knitting stitches

Spacing of design elements

When you decide to make a yarn with a repeating design element — a knot, a slub, or a dip dyed sequence — you will need to decide how to space your repeats. How much space should occur between elements? Should the texture or color occur regularly, or at random? Your decisions will depend in part on how you plan to use the yarn — a good reason for designing the project before the yarn!

The same yarn will have very different effects when woven, knitted, or crocheted. Weaving is linear. Knitting and crochet are looped structures; a given length of yarn doesn't travel as great a distance in the finished fabric as it would if it were woven. For example, 12 inches of yarn would provide 12 inches of woven warp or weft, but might work into 4 inches of knitted stitches. This example indicates that if you make a knot yarn and put the knots 12 inches apart, the knots will occur every 12 inches in a woven fabric and every 4 inches in a knitted one.

Samples are typically much smaller than finished projects, so the patterns of repeating elements won't look the same in your sample as they do when you work "for real." It is easier to predict what a fabric will look like from a sample if the design elements are randomly spaced in the yarn. If you choose regular placement, you may be in for some rude surprises, depending on the placement interval and the dimensions of your project.

In knitting, for example, you may want to make a sweater in the round, using a slub yarn. The slubs occur every 15 inches. When you begin to work, it turns out that the amount of yarn used in one round of the sweater is an even multiple of 15 inches. You'll find yourself with vertical ridges of slubs in your knitted fabric. In weaving, you may decide to make a dip dyed yarn for warp. It is mostly blue, with a white section that repeats every 18 inches. The warp length is 72 inches (an even multiple of 18), so as you measure the warp you find an ikat-like block of white every 18 inches.

In order to produce a random placement of the dominant color or texture within a fabric, you need to place the color or texture randomly in the yarn. Sometimes enjoyable and surprising patterns evolve from the overlapping of colors in a space-dyed yarn. However, if you don't like what you're seeing you can alter the effect in the finished product if you periodically remove a section of yarn to change the repeat — or modify the pattern by changing the number of stitches in your knitting repeat or swapping certain warp yarns' positions.

The spacing of design elements may not be apparent from your sample

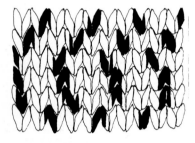

The same yarn will appear to have more closely spaced design elements if it is knitted than if it is woven.

Yarn for garments

Special considerations, such as warmth/coolness and softness/durability, come into play when we design yarns to be used in garments. My first handwoven item (after a

---

YARN DESIGN. The bottom swatch is a beautiful yarn, but its horizontal color pattern fights with the vertical cable. A similar knitted structure at the top works better with a simpler color effect. The swatch at center right was made from a two-ply slub. The fabric is bumpier on its purl side.

sampler made in a workshop) was a wool scarf. It was lovely, except that I made the serious mistake of using mill-end rug yarns. I could only stand to have it around my neck for about 15 minutes.

If you will be lining the garment or using it for outerwear, almost any fiber can be used. A fabric which will be worn next to the skin must be soft.

Test fabrics for "wearability"

People have different tolerances for softness or scratchiness. Sometimes a fabric will feel soft to the hand, but after several hours of wear around the neck it can feel like steel wool. You can test for "wearability" with your sample. Place it inside your collar, next to your skin, and keep it there for a couple of hours. If it still feels comfortable at the end of that time, it is likely to feel good all day.

Promising candidates for "next-to-the-skin" fibers feel soft and are fine in diameter. Wool is the most controversial fiber in this regard. The coarseness or softness of wool varies radically, depending upon the breed it comes from. Wool from breeds known for fine-diameter, soft fibers can be used next to the skin. Don't evaluate a fleece's softness by feeling it in the grease; a fresh fleece can feel softer than it actually is because of the lanolin. Wash it, test it, and then evaluate it.

Fine fibers such as qiviut, angora, camel down, silk, and cashmere are known for their luxurious softness. Other possibilities for next-to-the-skin garments include all of the vegetable fibers (linen, ramie, cotton, and so on), goat down (not hair), some dog hair, and kid mohair.

Do you want to be warm or cool?

If you want to feel either warm or cool in your garment, your choices of fiber and of yarn preparation techniques will help you. If you want to stay cool, vegetable fibers are usually best, since they're absorbent. Perspiration is one of the body's cooling mechanisms. If the moisture builds up on our skin, we feel hotter. If it is removed (absorbed by our clothing), we feel more comfortable.

For warmth, we need insulation just as a house does. Insulation in a building often consists of dead air space. Warm yarns contain insulating air, too. Woolen yarns trap more air — and so keep you toastier — than worsted yarns.

Wind resistance also affects our ability to stay warm. A garment that keeps the wind out will make us feel warmer. The tightness of a fabric's structure has a lot to do with its ability to keep out drafts. For example, a sweater knitted of fine yarn on very small needles can be warmer than one made of thick yarn worked loosely. Fulling (or felting) fills the air spaces between fibers, so fulled fabrics are more wind-resistant than are non-fulled fabrics.

Warp yarn

I'm sure you've heard that handspun cannot be used as warp. Well, the people who perpetuate that myth are wrong. I've had my share of troubles with handspun yarn —more on that in a moment—but the difficulties can be predicted and easily dealt with.

The problems that occur in handspun warp are:
- weak spots that may break under warp tension
- abrasion by the reed and heddles which frays the yarn
- adjacent warps which stick together, making it difficult to get a good shed

Problems with handspun warp

I once wove a throw with handspun warp and weft that had all of these problems. It was my first "major" piece of weaving, and sampling never occurred to me. I put a 45-inch-wide, 2½-yard warp on the loom. Some of the thicker areas in the warp yarn didn't fit through the reed too well. With each beat, the fat part was pulled and abraded. In addition, the warp was sticky. The warp ends would latch onto their neighbors like their lives depended on it. I tried hairspray. I tried spray starch. I tried this stuff called "Weave All." Nothing worked.

I let the loom sit there for six months with six inches woven, hoping the fairies would come in and fix it all up for me. They never came.

Finally, I managed to weave off the whole warp using a three-inch tapestry fork to beat the yarn in, instead of the beater. It was slow going, but I did get that "dog" off the loom, and it turned out beautifully.

Now let me tell you how not to make these mistakes.

It is easy to spin a yarn that is strong enough to withstand the tension of weaving. How strong the warp must be depends on how much tension will be used. For example, a handspun rug warp must be much sturdier than handspun for a delicate scarf. Spin relatively smoothly and evenly (you can put in texture, but make sure it will *stay* there). Be certain you have enough twist in your yarn. Consider plying.

Strength and slubs

If you have a slub in the yarn that is slightly larger than the dents in your reed, you are in trouble. When you beat, the slub will catch in the reed and the yarn will be stretched out like a rubber band, only it won't bounce back. This tug-

ging pulls out fibers, in addition to extending and weakening the yarn. The yarn will become thin and then it will break near the slub. Know what reed you will use, and watch the size of your slubs (both length, to withstand the loom's tension, and width, for the reed's abrasion).

To minimize reed abrasion problems, use a reed with few dents per inch. Eight dents per inch will work if the yarn isn't too thick; 4 or 5 dents to the inch is better. If your yarn is not fuzzy, just knotty, you can reduce abrasion by using a reed with half as many teeth per inch by putting two warp ends in each slot. This leaves wider gaps for each knot to go through.

Heddle abrasion cannot be reduced much, but you can check to see that the heddles are large enough to accommodate the yarn. String heddles are sometimes kinder to a fragile warp than steel heddles. Wire heddles fall in between.

The sticky-warp problem can be solved in a couple of ways, despite my earlier failure to discover answers. When you change sheds, the yarns want to stay attached to their neighbors. If you are weaving plain weave on a four-harness jack loom, thread to a straight twill and have one treadle attached to each harness. To make a new shed, press first one treadle and then the other. The yarns will separate more easily.

You can reduce stickiness and gain some power against reed abrasion by sizing your warp. I try to avoid this, since it's messy and the sized yarn feels so stiff and lifeless—although the size washes out after the fabric has been woven. You can purchase commercial warp size, or use a home brew.

WARP SIZE

Mix 8 tablespoons of white flour with a bit of cold water to make a paste. Add 2 quarts of boiling water, stir, and allow to cool.

Dip the warp chain in the size and allow it to absorb the fluid. Squeeze it out slightly and hang it to dry. After it's dry, dress the loom.

Stickiness and abrasion can also be reduced if you spin the yarn with some extra twist, and let your fingers smooth down loose fibers as the yarn passes by on its way to the

---

COORDINATED YARNS. The two yarns at left are singles; the solid color was used for the body of the sweater and the heathered blend for its ribbing. A two-ply, made of handspun singles with contrasting slubs plied with commercial thread, makes a lovely vest.

bobbin. Set the twist on this yarn by wrapping it onto a reel, niddy noddy, or warping board and steaming it with a clothing steamer, instead of by washing it. Keep the yarn under some tension until you have finished weaving. After you wash the finished fabric, the yarn will soften and fill out.

Coordinated yarns

Handspinners, unlike mills, can create complementary yarns, to be used together in one project. The possibilities are limited only by your imagination. If you use coordinated yarns, your work will be more individual and even more special. Here are some ideas:

—Spin two different but related two-ply yarns for a sweater which will have stripes. If one yarn is made of colors A and B and the other of colors A and C, both subtlety and contrast occur.

—Use two colors of dyed fiber to spin two yarns, then blend the colors to make a third yarn which ties the original colors together.

—Spin different sizes of yarn to be used in different parts of a garment, or in coordinating separates. For a bulky sweater, a lighter yarn may provide a more supple and comfortable ribbing.

—Make a variegated yarn and use it with a solid-colored yarn in one of the component colors.

Dyeing fleece or yarn?

Adding color can be done at any stage of yarn-making. Your decisions will again depend on the final yarn you want, and how you want the color to appear in your finished project. Some of your choices are to dye raw fiber, processed fiber such as roving or top, or finished yarn. We'll consider the possibilities in more depth later.

SPINNING CONTROL

Yarn size

Yarn thickness or *grist* is a basic design feature. One of the first things you want to be able to do is spin whatever thickness of yarn you want. The factors which influence yarn thickness include:

the diameter and length of the fibers
the density of the fiber preparation
the drafting method
the wheel's drive ratio
the sizes of the orifice and the flyer hooks

Short fibers work most easily and securely into fine yarns. To make sure that each individual fiber is fastened into the yarn, you need to spin a yarn that twists every fiber around several times. When you spin short fibers into a thick yarn, they aren't caught firmly enough in the twist. If you really want a thick yarn and are working with short fibers, spin several finer yarns and ply them together. A thick yarn with enough twist to hold short fibers securely in place would be drastically overtwisted.

Fine fibers, with small diameters, also do better in fine yarns, as coarse fibers suit thicker yarns. For example, use Merino for a gossamer shawl and Border Leicester for a heavy rug yarn.

Dense fiber preparations make the spinning of thick yarns easier; a thick yarn occurs when the twist secures more fiber in each revolution, and a dense preparation makes a big chunk of fiber available. Try spinning from different densities of batts or rolags to compare your results. If you have a dense fiber preparation and want to spin a fine yarn, separate the batt or roving into small sections and spin from them.

If you prepare and spin your fiber with the woolen techniques, the yarn will be fatter (and lighter in weight) than if you use worsted techniques.

A low-ratio wheel with a big bobbin, orifice, and flyer hooks will most easily make a thick, low-twist yarn. A high-ratio wheel with a small bobbin, orifice, and flyer hooks will work best for a fine, high-twist yarn.

Yarn grist can be expressed as the number of yards per

Factors which influence
yarn thickness

pound, or can be gauged by the number of yarns that can be wrapped side-by-side in a given space (usually an inch). Two yarns which appear to be the same size can have different grists, depending on the way they were spun. A woolen yarn, for instance, contains more air than a worsted yarn of the same apparent thickness and so will have more yards per pound. You can measure grist in a number of ways.

Wrap the yarn into a **skein of known circumference**. Count the number of wraps and multiply by the circumference to get the total number of yards in the skein. Weigh the skein and divide the number of yards by the weight (expressed as a fraction of a pound) to discover how many yards are in a pound of this yarn.

An easier way to answer the same question is to use a **McMorran Yarn Balance**. Spin a sample of yarn and *set the twist*. Place it across the balance beam. Trim the ends of the sample a little at a time until the beam balances in its notches. Measure the remaining sample (in inches) and multiply this number by 100 — voila! Yards per pound! (The McMorran Yarn Balance also comes in a metric version.)

Because the twist must be set and the yarn completely dry for this device to work, you can use the McMorran Balance at two different stages in the design-and-spinning process, for two different reasons. If you are planning a project, you can measure your sample. In this case, you can adjust your spinning technique, if necessary, based on the information you get. If you have already spun up all your yarn, you will be able to figure out whether you've got enough to complete a weaving or knitting project.

A useful measure for spinning consistent yarns involves **wrapping a sample strand** around a rod, ruler, or piece of cardboard for an inch and counting the number of wraps. This won't give you an arbitrary number, like yards per pound; it will give you a relative number which you can use for comparisons.

A fine yarn will produce more wraps (say, 20) than a thick yarn (say, 8). You can make or buy a small wooden "inch gauge" to use in making these tests. Be sure that as you wrap yarn on your gauge you aren't removing twist.

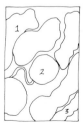

SIMPLE TWO-PLY YARNS. Even the most basic structure can be elegant. (1) Samoyed plied with silk. (2) Handspun silk plied with commercial silk. (3) Variegated hand-dyed commercial silk singles plied with two-ply silk thread. The other skeins and balls are various combinations of two strands.

Twist

If it weren't for twist, there would be no spinning wheels. A spinning wheel is simply a device that twists. Twist makes fibers into yarn; well-controlled twist makes them into sound yarn. Often we just put in whatever twist the wheel seems to give us, without considering how much twist or what type of twist would be best for the yarn we're making.

The first thing to know about twist is its **direction**. Let's clarify the S and Z business of twist. When I finally figured it out, I couldn't believe it was so simple. A single strand of yarn is spun with the wheel spinning in one direction or the other. The direction that the wheel was spinning makes a yarn S or Z. S or Z is just another way of saying *right* or *left*. To identify a yarn as having S or Z twist, look at the angle of the twist and see if it is going in the same direction as the middle part of the letter S or Z. The direction of twist is the same if you are looking at a yarn upside down or backward. Try turning a yarn upside down to see for yourself.

As neat as this trick is, it isn't especially interesting or helpful all by itself. However, it becomes useful when you realize how profoundly it affects yarn design.

Different directions of twist give yarns different appearances. If you spin yarn for a weft-faced weaving, some with S twist and some with Z but otherwise identical, your finished fabric will look different where you switch from S yarn to Z yarn. This could be done on purpose, but could also be suboptimal if you do it unwittingly.

Twist becomes fascinating when you want to start plying. Just as spinning can take place in the S or Z direction, plying also occurs in either the S or Z direction. If you ply in the same direction that you spun, you will *add* twist to your yarn. If you ply in the opposite direction, you will *remove* twist. If you know the direction of twist of yarn A and yarn B, you can decide whether your plying will *add* or *remove* twist from either or both of these strands.

The other important aspect of twist, besides the direction, is its **amount**. This can be expressed as twists per inch, or as the angle of twist.

Twists per inch can be measured in a singles yarn in two ways. You can take a strand of *freshly spun* yarn, double it, let it ply back on itself, and count the number of plying twists in an inch. This number doubled will give you the approximate number of twists per inch in your single strand. A more accurate way to count twists per inch is to

S-twist Z-twist

Twist in plying

Measuring twists per inch

Spinning Control

mark a one-inch length of yarn with two straight pins, inserted crosswise in the strand. Hold the pins. Rotate one pin and untwist the yarn, counting each full revolution of the pin. When all the twist between the two pins is removed, you will have a number that represents the twists per inch that were in the yarn.

The angle of twist is much easier to measure, and is more helpful when you want to keep the twist consistent while you spin. Place a protractor under the yarn and measure the angle of twist.

Measuring the angle of twist

The lower limit on twist is just enough to get the fiber to hang together, while the upper limit is so much that the yarn kinks up. In between, there is an ideal level of twist for a particular yarn. As we've noted, fine yarns and short fibers need more twist, while thick yarns and longer fibers need less.

How much twist?

In general, yarns with more twist are stronger — up to a certain point, where they become brittle. A weaving yarn to be used as warp needs more twist than one which will be used as weft. Yarns with less twist are lighter, softer, and warmer, because they incorporate more air space.

Fiber preparation

There are many ways to prepare fiber for spinning, and the preparation method strongly influences the finished yarn. You can spin directly from a greasy lock of wool, or you can use commercially prepared combed top, or any of the stages in between. In general, the more uniform and even the fiber preparation, the smoother the finished yarn will be. Conversely, uneven preparations result in textured yarns.

Gorgeous textured yarns which emphasize the curly fibers of such wool breeds as Lincoln and Teeswater can be spun directly from lightly teased locks. In this way the locks retain their natural formation, instead of being disrupted by carding.

Teasing — pulling apart clumps in the fibers to make a uniformly fluffy mass — is the first step of fiber preparation for woolen spinning. It can be done by hand, or with one of the mechanical "pickers." The pickers speed the task considerably. You can run fibers through more than once for more uniform results and to blend fibers and colors.

Teasing

You can follow teasing with carding, which includes both short and long fibers evenly distributed within the fiber mass. The carded batt or rolag eliminates the parallel align-

Carding

ment of fibers in favor of loosening, fluffing, and blending the locks. You can card with handcards or a drum carder. For the smoothest yarns from carded wool, you may want to do the initial carding on coarse cloth and a final carding on finer cloth. To check your progress, take the batt or rolag and hold it up to the light. Any unevenness will show up as a clump or dark area.

Combing

Combing starts with individual, unteased locks. In the combing process, all of the short fibers are removed and the remaining long fibers end up in a highly organized parallel arrangement. You can buy combed wool, or you can prepare your own by using wool combs, or by using a small carder or dog brush to comb the shorter fibers out of individual locks. If you are serious about combing, you will need a serious set of combs. They allow you to process larger quantities of combed fiber faster and your results will be more precise.

Mill preparations

Handspinners have access to a wide variety of mill preparations. You can save a great deal of time by purchasing some of these, since the fibers don't need to be washed and carded or combed before you start to spin. Buying mill preparations, though, compromises your control over the final result by making preparation decisions for you.

Some of the terms you'll encounter when you look for mill-prepared fibers are *batts, roving, sliver,* and *top.* **Batts** are carded sheets, similar to those you can produce on a drum carder at home. They're larger, since they come from a bigger set of carding drums. **Roving, sliver,** and **top** are terms for mill preparations which will provide the spinner with a continuous flow of fibers.

Woolen or worsted?

Develop a repertoire of drafting styles so that you can match your spinning technique to the fiber preparation you're working with and to the yarn you want to produce. A long draw, where an arm's length of fiber is drafted out as the twist enters it, will yield a relatively smooth, uniformly twisted yarn from a carded preparation, while a short "push-pull" draft allows the opportunity to insert slubs at controlled intervals.

COLOR BLENDS. Blending can be thorough or not, for different effects. (1) Relatively homogeneous blends of various colors and fibers. (2) Less thorough blends. (3) Rough blends. (4) Small skeins of black, white, and two grays—one roughly blended and one thoroughly blended.

Combed preparations can be drafted in the classic worsted manner, where short, uniform lengths are drawn out and the twist is inserted in a controlled way so all the fibers are smoothly caught and held in place. Or you can take combed fibers and pull off short segments, fold them over your index finger, and draft from the fold.

If you haven't mastered these and other drafting techniques, workshops and other spinning books will help you become more versatile so you can play more with yarn design.

Consistency

For a project, you'll want the last yarn you spin to be the same in size and twist as the first yarn. When you spin a large batch of yarn, it's easy to slowly change the yarn's diameter or amount of twist without meaning to.

Make a guide!

Make yourself a guide. Spin a length of the yarn you want and wrap it around a piece of cardboard, under tension. You don't want to wash it or set the twist first. Periodically compare your newly spun yarn to this reference sample.

Keep a protractor handy. Compare the angle of twist now and then.

You'll find that your eye is surprisingly accurate in helping you spin consistently when it has reference points. Add each sample to your notebook, along with records of fiber preparation and spinning procedures, for future reference.

Spinning Control

COLOR

If you aren't already an avid dyer, I hope that you will be inspired to become one by the end of this chapter or, at the very least, by the end of the book. I'll give you some general information on dyeing, as well as some ideas on how to use basic techniques in unusual ways to get unique, exciting results.

Why dye?

Color! Color is often the first thing that attracts us to home furnishings, garments, or works of art. It is an important design element in any project. Your "design power" greatly increases if you dye your own fibers, since you can create exactly the color you want. There are so many reasons to dye that it's hard to know where to start.

One benefit of dyeing is that you can reduce your inventory of spinning fibers and of yarns. You buy only natural-colored fiber, then dye the quantity you need for a particular project. This saves both money and space.

Often, spinners must dye the fibers themselves in order to get specific colors, since most unspun fibers are available only in natural shades. The market is changing somewhat, now that "rainbow batts" and other dyed preparations are appearing, but the colors for sale may not be the ones you want.

If you are doing your own dyeing you can use techniques which produce unique combinations of color. In variegated or rainbow dyeing, several colors are applied to a single batch of fiber, so the different colors are adjacent to each other.

Dyeing and color blending provide valuable opportunities to experiment with and learn about color. It's also a lot more fun to work with fluffy, rainbow-hued piles of fiber! In addition, I think that my final products look more "finished" and less "home-made" if I have control over every step in their production.

Dye types

You will choose first between natural and synthetic dyes. For years, I was an avid natural dyer. I later discovered that

Dyeing can be economical; it also gives you flexibility

I prefer synthetic dyes for several reasons. They are faster to use, their color range is unlimited, they cost less, and all of the variegated dyeing methods work with them.

There are three basic kinds of synthetic dyes which I use: union dyes, acid dyes, and alkaline dyes. Brand names come and go, but most readily available dyes fit into one of these categories.

Union dyes, or household dyes, offer a combination of acid and alkaline dyes. Common brand names are Rit® and Cushing®. These dyes can be easily used on either cellulose or protein fibers, but are fairly expensive. Their light- and washfastness are better on protein fibers than on cellulose, although not fantastic on either. Because they are readily available, you can become familiar with dyeing by using them.

Both acid and alkaline dyes have better light- and washfastness than union dyes. However, each of these types works only on certain fibers.

Acid dyes color protein fibers such as wool and silk. The dye "takes" in the presence of a mild acid solution. They are the primary dyes for protein fibers, like wool. Since handspinners work with protein fibers more frequently than cellulose fibers, these dyes are used a lot. Several types are available: the "kiton" or leveling, milling, supermilling, and pre-metallized dyes. Specific names include Ciba Kiton, Lanaset®, and Cibalan®. These dyes usually come in powder form in black and primary colors. Powder for secondary colors is sometimes available. More subtle colors are prepared by blending dyes.

Mixing colors is easy if you keep on hand *stock solutions* of the primary colors and a toner like black. You can make a stock solution by mixing a measured amount of dye powder with water. Each solution can then be measured into the dyepot by the drop, for very pale hues, or by the tablespoon or milliliter, for more intense colors. By measuring carefully and keeping track of your recipes, you can reproduce colors with great reliability. A 1 percent solution is good for starters.

YARNS DYED FOR COLOR EFFECTS. These are all silk noil and silk top. The small tufts of fiber were dyed and then spun. The large skein was spun, then dyed.

After a while, slimy stuff may develop in the jars. I ignore it and use the dye and get good results.

Heat and *acid* are essential to set acid dyes properly. Sometimes the instructions show elaborate techniques involving other chemicals, specific amounts of time, and precise temperatures. These directions will help you avoid streaking; if you want evenly colored yarn, pay attention. I have to confess that I like streaky yarn, and streaks in unspun fiber create no problem since they'll be blended out later anyway. So I usually simplify the directions, as you'll see later on when we discuss dyeing fiber (pages 36-37).

I make sure that the fiber simmers for at least half an hour, and that the solution in which the dyeing occurs is acidic—do follow the directions that come with the dyes for the amounts of acid to use. If these critical elements are controlled, the dyes will be fast.

Alkaline dyes (also known as *fiber reactive* dyes) work in a different pH environment—no acids here!—and they color vegetable fibers, although many also work on silk. Many of these dyes do not require heat. Stock solutions of these dyes do not store well, so mix a new set from powder each time you dye. Their wash- and lightfastness are outstanding; unlike the fibers to which they are applied, they don't tolerate chlorine bleach. Some dyes of this type are Procion® (marketed under a variety of names, including Fibrec®) and Cibacron F®.

The basic instructions require that you soak the fiber in a salt solution for 10 minutes, then add the dissolved dye and stir frequently for 30 minutes, and finally add washing soda[1] (the alkaline part) for 45 minutes, to set the dye. Darker colors require more salt; the amount of salt can be between 20 and 110 percent of the fiber weight. Washing soda is 10

---

[1]Sodium carbonate. The kind in the grocery store used to work, but has now been so "improved" for laundry purposes that we can no longer depend on it for dyeing. You'll need to get it from a chemical or dye supply company.

percent of fiber weight. Dissolve it in hot water before you add it to the dyebath.

Most synthetic dyes are toxic (as are many of the mordants and some of the dyestuffs in natural dyeing), and you should be careful to follow the safety precautions recommended for each type. In most cases, the greatest hazards come from the airborne particles (the powder that blows around when you mix stock solutions) and the vapors (from the heating dyepot), so a mask or, better, a respirator is a must during these parts of the process. Wear gloves so no dye gets on your skin. And *don't* use your kitchen utensils or containers for dyeing, and vice versa.

Safety precautions

Dyeing raw fiber

Dyeing raw fiber is not the same as dyeing yarn. The drier tips and the cut ends of the material—dog hair, fleece, unspun silk, or what-have-you—take up the dye differently. The tips usually end up darker, but sometimes they turn an entirely different color. Often yarn which you spin from dyed fiber will look a little heathered, even if you did all the dyeing in the same dyebath.

I usually store fleeces clean, and wash them soon after I acquire them. I use my washing machine as a tub, but I *never allow the machine to agitate.* Before I run water into the machine, I remove all the fleece. I gently return the fiber to the washer after the water level is where I want it. I let the fleece soak with lots of liquid dishwashing detergent for about half an hour. Then I gently move the fleece around with a plunger. The machine's spin-only cycle whirls out the dirty water. This procedure is repeated twice more, with plain warm water, for rinsing. I am told that using my washing machine this way isn't great for it, although I've been doing this for a long time and so far haven't had any trouble.

Storing and washing fleeces

My method works well for medium to coarse fibers. I recommend a gentler process—for instance, hand washing smaller batches in a sink or bathtub, without squeezing or agitating the fibers—for finer fleeces.

To dye fleece using acid dyes, you can begin with clean or greasy fleece, wet or dry. The results vary with each of these choices, but success can be had from any of them. (Dye formula calculations are most accurate if you consistently work with clean fiber.) Gather a clump of fiber of the desired weight (always *dry* weight) and tie it into a rectangular piece of cheesecloth. Pull the opposite corners of the

Using acid dyes on fleece

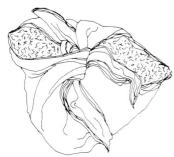

Cheesecloth contains fibers in a dyebath

A stop bath gives you control

cheesecloth together and knot them, so the fibers are contained but loose.

Prepare your dyebath with dye, acid, and any other ingredients you may be using. Add the fleece. Simmer the fiber in the dyebath until the water is clear and the dye has been exhausted. If the color is not quite right, remove the fiber, add more dye, replace the fiber, and continue to simmer. The fiber should simmer at least 30 minutes to set the dye.

If you like the color early in the processing, when there is still dye in the water, you can remove the fiber from the dyebath and simmer it in a separate pot of plain water and acid for a total of 30 to 45 minutes. This "stop bath" must be at the same temperature as the dyebath when you put the fiber into it. Otherwise your fleece will felt.

After a dyebath is exhausted, I often recycle its water for another batch of fiber. This saves both energy and time. I add more dye and a little acid and start over.

If you find yourself using a lot of acid dyes, you may go through a lot of acetic acid in the form of vinegar. Glacial acetic acid, which can be obtained from a photographic supply house, is more economical but must be diluted. Vinegar is 5 percent acid and glacial acetic acid is 100 percent acid, so use 1/20 as much. *Always* work with good ventilation and *always* add the acid to the water, not vice versa.

To dye cellulose fibers using fiber reactive dyes, begin with dry fiber. For consistent results, weigh the dry fiber and record the amounts of dye, salt, and soda that you use.

Certain colors of fiber reactive dyes require heat

Put the fiber in loose cheesecloth bags, and add just enough warm water to cover. Remove the wet fiber and add dissolved plain table salt (20 to 110 percent of fiber weight, depending on desired depth of shade). Put the wet fiber back into the dyebath and leave it there for ten minutes. Remove the fiber, add the dye, return the fiber to the pot, and leave it for thirty minutes. You can stir gently to help distribute the dye evenly, or leave it unstirred if you want to get different shades of color from the same dyebath. Turquoise and black fiber reactive dyes require heat (simmering temperature for the rest of this procedure) while other colors do not, so heat at this point if you are using those dyes. After 30 minutes, lift out the fiber and add dissolved washing soda (10 percent of fiber weight) to the pot. Return the fiber and stir occasionally for 45 more minutes.

You'll need to rinse your newly dyed fibers. Otherwise excess dye will end up on your hands when you're spinning. If I am dyeing several batches of fiber, I cool the fiber and then place all the batches in one large tub for a mass wash-and-rinse. After rinsing, I use the washing machine's spin-only cycle to remove excess water. The fiber dries a lot faster then. Wool can be teased or picked while damp; this also promotes faster drying.

Rinse all newly dyed fibers

Modified techniques can help when you dye silk. I do not use cheesecloth to enclose silk during dyeing. This fiber often accepts dye so quickly that sometimes it's best not to use any acid, and to start with fiber in a dyebath at room temperature. Slowly increase the temperature of the dyebath. When silk dries it often becomes stiff, but the stiffness will disappear as you spin.

Colors are always lighter when the fiber is dry than when it's wet. If you don't like a color you have produced, you can always overdye it or blend it with something else. In case of total disaster, you can remove dye with a color stripper like sodium hydrosulfite (Rit® Color Remover) or thiorea dioxide.

Dyeing yarn

Skein yarn and tie it in at least four places around the skein before you dye it. Longer skeins will need more ties. If you will dye several skeins together in one dyebath, you can tie them together with a loop of yarn. Leave the end of the loop hanging outside the dyepot so you can easily lift them out together. You can also hold onto this loop and swish the yarn through the dyebath, as a form of stirring.

Skein yarn or roving before you dye it

To avoid streaks, begin with thoroughly wet fiber. Be sure there's enough liquid in your dyebath so the fiber can move freely, raise the temperature slowly, and stir regularly. As mentioned above, lift the yarn out before you add more dye, stir the dye to spread it evenly through the liquid, and then return the yarn to the dyebath. Rinse as for raw fiber.

You can skein and dye roving, as well. Because the roving has a tendency to felt, and can then be difficult or impossible to spin, be careful not to agitate it much and don't heat it more than the minimum amount of time required for fastness. Interesting space-dyeing effects work particularly well on roving.

I use a digital wristwatch with a timer for dyeing. I set it to beep me every 20 minutes so I can check the pots. I am sure it has helped keep my house from burning down when I might have forgotten my dyepots.

Color theory

Before we get very far with adding color to our fibers, we need to think at least briefly about color theory. Some people seem to have an innate sense about color which enables them to use it easily and well. Whether or not you are blessed with this gift, the more you learn about color the better you will be at predicting what happens when you put colors and patterns together.

Sources of inspiration

There are many wonderful sources of color inspiration. Keep a notebook of design ideas. Cut out magazine photos. Truly look at the works of your favorite artists — mine include Van Gogh, Paul Klee, and Robert and Sonia Delaunay. Try nature photography, from your own efforts or from books. Analyze color combinations which appeal to you and see if you can discover what they have in common. Play with color. Arrange combinations with paint chips or color fans. Mix water colors (they'll help you feel more comfortable combining dyes). Get a computer program that lets you draw or "paint" on the color monitor.

If you're hesitant about color, I encourage you to reread this section once a week for ten weeks. It took me about two years before the concepts really sank in. The information is so useful I wish I had "gotten it" sooner.

The ideas presented here are not intended to be rules you must follow, but a foundation from which you can start working with color or from which you can experiment with new possibilities. Please keep in mind that the color of a yarn must ultimately work in a finished project.[2] Some of the guidelines apply to finished projects, some to yarn only. I'll first provide some definitions of basic terms, then go on to talk about color schemes and general principles of color use.

Color terms

Hue: The attribute of a color by which it is distinguished from another. All colors are judged to be similar to one or

---

[2]Although some skeins are so beautiful you'll just want to keep them intact. A friend once gave me some Samoyed dog hair and I made a gorgeous variegated single which I plied with silk. I gave her a small skein of the yarn; she later told me she kept it with her always. On bad days she would take it out of her purse and look at it to calm herself down. How's that for yarn therapy?

Color

two of the spectral hues (the primary and secondary colors): red, blue, yellow, orange, green, or purple. Black and white lack hue.

Primary colors: The basic colors which together can mix a wide range of colors, but which cannot themselves be mixed. The two sets of primaries frequently encountered in dyeing are red, blue, and yellow, or magenta, turquoise (cyan), and yellow.

Secondary colors: Those colors which are produced by mixing two of the primaries: orange, green, and purple.

Color wheel: A circle which presents a progression of colors, usually including the twelve basic hues: yellow, yellow-orange, orange, red-orange, red, red-violet, purple, blue-violet, blue, blue-green, green, yellow-green.

Color sphere (or *color cone*): A three-dimensional expansion of the color wheel which includes *shades* and *tints* as well as pure hues. This concept provides a better overall idea of how color mixing works.

Intensity: The measurable brightness of a color; synonymous with *saturation*. The colors around the color wheel or on the "equator" of the color sphere are pure hues of high intensity. For example, royal blue is more intense than pale blue.

Tints: Pure hues combined with white create tints, which are inherently harmonious because they all have white in common. Tints have a springlike, youthful, unsophisticated connotation.

Shades: Pure hues combined with black create shades. They are dark, rich, and dignified.

Tones: Pure hues combined with gray. They are refined, winter-like, muted, subtle, and show restraint. They go well together and have a natural affinity for gray, which is one of their components.

Value: The lightness or darkness of a color is its value. A lighter color is higher in value. Tints therefore have higher value than shades.

Warm and cool colors: Red, orange, and yellow are considered "warm" colors, while green, blue, and purple are classified as "cool."

Color schemes

Monochromatic: A color scheme which is based on one hue—for example, blue. This is a very safe scheme, since the hue pulls everything together, but it can be a bit boring and staid. A monochromatic color scheme based on blue could include tints, tones, shades, and intense blues. Monochromatic color schemes also frequently incorporate some neutral colors (white, black, or gray).

Analogous: A color scheme based on hues which are adjacent in a traditional color wheel. One example would be green, blue, and purple. Another would be purple and red. Tints, shades, and tones are fair game. This scheme is easy to use and works well with a dash of another hue to jazz it up. The idea is particularly effective in rainbow batts. It's still pretty safe, but has more room for play than a monochromatic scheme.

Complementary: A color scheme founded on hues which lie directly opposite each other on the color wheel. Examples are red and green, yellow and purple, or orange and blue. These combinations can be very exciting, but are more challenging to pull off successfully. They are full of conflict. One way to smooth the path is to use all tints, tones, or shades. Instead of red and green, you could use pink and celery, or instead of orange and blue you could try rust and navy. If purer hues are used, more excitement is created. Can you handle it? Do you want it?

Neutrals: A color scheme built around white, gray, black, tan, and brown is easy to work with, but can be overly sober and restrained. The absence of intense hue unites these colors. Spice this combination up, if you want, by introducing elements of a supplementary monochromatic, analogous, or complementary scheme.

Variegated dyeing

Variegated dyeing, multicolor dyeing, and *rainbow dyeing* are all terms which refer to the finished look of dyed fiber (raw fiber, roving, or yarn) which contains several colors in one dyelot. *Space-dyeing* is also used to refer to one type of variegated dyeing process. The effect can be achieved in a variety of ways: by dipping sections of a skein of yarn into a dyebath or series of dyebaths, or by applying different colors of dye solution or powder to fiber (rainbow, variegated, or multicolor dyeing).

Variegated dyeing is spontaneous and fun, and you get truly unique results. It is possible to keep track of the amounts of dye you use and to replicate the results, but this is one area where I'll go against my own advice. I find it's a lot more fun to be serendipitous with this type of dyeing and not keep track of anything!

Plan your color combinations with one eye on basic color theory. Analogous schemes are usually successful; often a

Variegated dyeing is fun, and gives unique results

bit of a "wilder" color will really perk a mixture up. Gather inspiration from all the sources previously mentioned and any others you come across. One way to see how colors will work together is to twist together yarns of the colors you are considering.

COLOR GUIDELINES

Some elementary guidelines will help you plan color effects. Some are particularly applicable to spinning and dyeing.

1. Lighter colors appear to come forward, dark colors to recede.

2. Warm colors also appear to come forward and cool colors to recede.

3. Carded batts appear to be lighter in color than will the finished yarn.

4. Rougher textures appear darker than smooth elements, because of the shadows.

5. Neutrals (gray, black, tan, and brown) can be created by combining three primaries. Shades and tones can be created by mixing complementary colors. Shades and tones made this way tend to look richer than those made by adding gray or black.

6. Optical mixing occurs when the eye blends two colors. This visual effect happens more easily when the colors are close in hue and value.

7. Colors will appear to mix more thoroughly at a distance than when viewed up close.

8. Colors with high contrast in hue or value will resist blending and it's hard to make them appear homogeneous.

9. Blends are richer and more interesting than flat planes of a single color.

Of the various variegated-dyeing methods, **dip-dyeing** most closely resembles the traditional techniques of dyeing yarn in a single color. Sections of a skein are dipped into a series of dyebaths so the colors alternate along its length. Skeined yarn, roving, and even measured warp chains can be dip dyed.

You can get three colors from two dyebaths if you allow the sections to overlap. For example, if you immerse two-thirds of a skein in a pink dyebath, then hold it from the opposite end and dip two-thirds in a blue dyebath, you will have a skein that includes pink, blue, and lavender sections (from the center third of the skein which went into both dyebaths).

Dip dyeing can give you three colors from two dyebaths

Workshop set-up

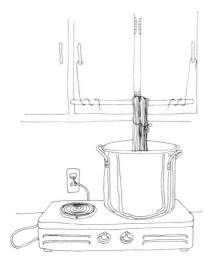

A simple arrangement with a dowel and some wire controls how much of these skeins enters the dyebath

In another variation, you can "fade" one color into another. This process is similar to the one described above, but on the second dyebath you raise the skein out of the dyebath in several steps so the intermediate area gradually changes from the color of the first dyebath to the color of the second.

I set up my workshop so a dowel is suspended over my dyepot. The height of the dowel above the pot is adjustable. I loop the skeins over the dowel and let them extend into the dyebath. If you can't make an arrangement like this, the part of the skein which you're not dyeing can hang over the edge of the pot—but put an extra container under it, because water (or dye liquid) will travel up the skein through a wicking action and needs a place to go.

One occasional disadvantage of dip dyeing is that the color repeats are quite regular. The yarn often looks better after it has been reskeined with a different skein diameter so the colors blend together. When you work with this yarn, an unintended pattern can show up in your fabric. Some of the other methods of variegated dyeing, which I'll describe shortly, produce more random results which eliminate this problem.

A plus in this type of dyeing is that you can record the recipe for each dyebath and then repeat your results. Figuring the strength of the dye solutions involves a little "seat of the pants" math. If you have a formula in your reference collection which represents one of the colors you want to obtain on a dip-dyed skein, you'll need to guess how much of your skein will be dyed with that color in order to know how much of the stock solution to put in that dyebath. For example, if about 66 percent (two-thirds) of your skein will be a bright rose color and you're working with a 100-gram skein, you'll make a dyepot which will dye 66 percent of a 100-gram skein (66 grams) to that color.

The other variegated-dyeing methods are related. They all allow you to use **direct application of dyes** to get more complexly colored and intricate results. The many variations depend on how much water is used, how the fiber is arranged, and how the dye is applied. The methods all involve applying different colors to different sections of fiber, within one dyebath or one dyeing process. Colors should be mixed from stock solutions before you apply them, and blended colors are more subtle and pleasing than pure stock solution hues.

You can work with raw fiber, roving, or yarn. I have used acid dyes extensively with these techniques, so my discus-

Color

sion will be based on this experience.

The amount of water is a critical element, since it determines how—and how much—the dye migrates through the fiber. Usually you'll want to restrict migration so the color areas will remain distinct.

One method uses just enough water to barely cover the fiber. It works well if you want to dye fleece which you will later use in color blends. Bright and distinctly different colors—like turquoise and magenta—are appropriate, since they will be well blended when you card.

Mix the colors you want from stock solutions. Pour each color where you want it on the fiber in the dyebath. You can easily use up to four different colors. Don't stir the dyebath, which will cause the colors to mix on the fiber. The longer the fiber remains in this type of dyebath the more the colors will migrate: it's amazing how much they'll travel in half an hour!

Another variation uses fiber which has been soaked and then squeezed out. Because there's even less water, migration of color will be minimized. If you want a little blending of colors, use a spray mister to apply extra water until the colors run a little. Some additional migration will occur when you set the color with steam or in the microwave.

For acid dyeing, soak the fiber in a mild acid solution, of the same strength recommended for the dyebath. After squeezing out the solution, lay the fiber on a large plastic garbage bag (so you won't get dye all over) and apply the dye as a liquid (you can spray it, pour it, or use a syringe) or as a powder.

The method which you use to apply the dye will greatly influence your results.

A spray bottle or airbrush can be used to apply stock solution. Unfortunately, the technique is messy, you need a way to catch the runoff, and the spray usually just coats the surface of the fiber with dye.

My favorite method of applying stock solutions involves syringes. You can get these tools from pharmacies; remove the needle, for safety. Special plastic syringes can be obtained from dye suppliers. They have longer tips and offer you more control in applying the dye.

With the syringe technique, you can get a larger number of distinct colors on a yarn or fiber. It's also easier to get dye into the center of a dense fiber mass, such as silk top. You can use the syringe in a low-water dyebath, as well as with soaked-and-squeezed fibers. When you work with a sy-

Dyeing with as little water as possible

Methods of applying dye

A syringe applies dye in distinct areas

Pouring dye produces more diffuse color patterns

ringe, you've also got a third option, although it only works for small quantities of fiber and it wastes some dye. You can lay the fiber in a strainer which fits inside a pot, apply the dye solution, and then steam the fiber over an acid/water solution.

Pouring the dye on can also give you any pattern you want. You can use the low-water bath or soaked-and-squeezed fibers. If you're determined, you may be able to approximately duplicate your results if you keep accurate records of fiber weight, amount of stock solution, and pouring pattern.

Sprinkling dye powder directly onto soaked fibers has some risks—both artistically and physically—but is good for getting lots of different colors onto one batch of fiber. The results aren't reproducible but the process is a lot of fun.

Because airborne dye powders are hazardous, you need to wear a respirator while working with this technique. The method also wastes dye because the powders usually don't all end up on the fiber.

Because the dye crystals look so insignificant on the fiber, you'll have trouble predicting your results. It's easy to get carried away and put too much powder on. Your fiber will then end up very dark.

The color begins to spread as soon as the dye powder gets wet. When you steam the fiber, the moisture in the steam will dissolve the powder and make the colors run somewhat.

Start with fiber which has been soaked in a weak acid bath. Salt and pepper shakers work well for sprinkling dye (use them *only* for dye once they've been used that way). Mix different dye powders in one shaker if you want, and use different shakers on different parts of the fiber.

The arrangement of your fibers will affect the dyeing

Once you know *how* you'll apply your dye, you can consider your fiber arrangement, which also influences the appearance of your finished product. The two factors to consider are the *density* of the fiber mass and its *arrangement*, as a skein, ball, or other collection.

Spread your fiber out so it isn't too thick in any one area; you want the dye to be able to penetrate to the center of the mass. Unspun fiber should be fluffed up. Longer skeins work better than short ones. Be especially careful with silk top, which is denser than other preparations.

Roving and skeins can be arranged in a number of patterns. You can wind them into circles for "pie dyeing" or snake them back and forth to get different results.

You can space-dye a ball of fiber, working with a tech-

Color

nique which resembles dip-dyeing. Prepare a *loose* ball with a ballwinder. Set up two different dyebaths which are deep enough to immerse only half to two-thirds of the ball. Place the ball in the first dyebath, then invert it and place it in the second. This method works best if you bring the temperature of the dyebaths up slowly; if the dye is absorbed too quickly, it will all be taken up by the outer layers and none will reach the ball's center.

Balls or cones of fiber can also be soaked in a weak acid solution and then shot full of different colors with syringes.

After you apply acid dyes, you need to set them with heat. You can steam the fibers in a large canning kettle on a stove, or put the yarn in a regular or microwave oven.

Alkaline dyes are set by leaving the soda/dye solution on the wet yarn for at least 60 minutes. Only turquoise and black need heat, so they can be set like acid dyes if you use one of the direct application techniques. Other colors can be set by mixing the soda with the dye before direct application, and then wrapping the dye-soaked fiber in plastic for an hour or more.

When you arrange the fiber before you set the dyes, be sure that it isn't doubled over on itself. The dyes could bleed from one section to another. You can prevent this bleeding by layering the fiber in a pot with intervening barriers of a plastic wrap which won't melt with the heat.

For stovetop steaming, place a rack in the bottom of a pot which has a little water in the bottom. Put the fiber on the rack and steam for between 45 and 60 minutes. Keep a lid on the pot to contain the heat and steam. The entire fiber mass must get hot, and it must stay hot for at least 30 minutes.

You can use a similar set-up with a conventional oven. A roaster pan with a rack and a lid works well. Keep the fiber moist while it is being heated.

In a microwave, layer the fiber and plastic wrap in a plastic bucket. Don't use a lid. Give the fiber a 5-minute zap on medium, let it sit for 5 minutes, repeat the 5-minute zap, let it rest for 5 more minutes, and finish with a third 5-minute zap.

EDITORIAL NOTE: The safety of using or setting dyes in closed appliances which are also used for food preparation (ovens and microwaves) has not been established. As always, any pots or utensils which you use in dyeing should be reserved for that purpose.

FIBER AND COLOR BLENDS

The infinite combinations possible in color and fiber blending can keep a spinner experimenting happily for years. The possibilities include:

- blending different colors to make heathered yarn
- adding small bits of felt or yarn to make tweeds or garnetted yarns
- combining color blending with fiber blending
- creating variegated or ombré yarns
- blending fibers to emphasize their desirable qualities

You can blend colors without having to do your own dyeing

Even if you don't dye your own fibers, there are many opportunities to add interest to your spinning through color blending techniques. You can blend naturally colored fleeces, or purchase dyed fiber or rainbow batts and rovings.

It's so exciting to experiment with different blends until you create a yarn you absolutely love. I have knitted samples of color-blended yarn that I like so much I keep them where I can gaze at them often, and dream about the wonderful sweater, mittens, or hat I will make some day.

Color blending

Why blend before spinning?

Why go to all this extra effort, when you can simply dye yarn a nice color after it has been spun? Because you can make luscious, unique yarns that cannot be found in any shop. Heathered yarns look much richer and more interesting than similar, solidly colored yarns. Color blending also gives you an excellent "hands on" opportunity to learn about color. If you admire the work of the Impressionist painters, you can explore their ideas in fiber. Besides, color blending doesn't have to take more time than simply dyeing yarn.

Color blending will also make your studio more efficient. You can use up small bits of fibers which have been around "too long." If you haven't got enough fleece or enough fiber of the same dyelot to complete a project, no problem—just blend in another color to "stretch" the main fiber. If you have some fiber of a not-quite-right color, you can modify it through blending. You may be pleasantly surprised by the results of combining all your leftovers. The most unlikely combinations can contribute to beautiful, original yarns.

Even if your results are ugly, you can overdye, use the yarn as a core for a new creation, or cut it into bits for garnetting. Remember that color blending works with exotic fibers as well as it does with the spinner's standby, wool.

You can mix as many colors together as you want, but keep in mind basic color theory when you plan blends. I usually experiment with blends by using hand cards, and then work out a procedure for making larger quantities on the drum carder.

Which colors, and how much of each?

My comments about experimentation notwithstanding, color choice in blending is one of the most significant factors in yarn design. Monochromatic blends are always safe, although they may be boring. Analogous blends are typically successful. Don't forget you can add neutrals, too.

An important aspect of designing blends involves the proportions in which each color appears. Often a small amount of a color which provides a contrast (in hue or value) will jazz up a blend. I often throw in a little magenta, turquoise, or bright red for pizzazz.

The **extent of your blending** will have a major effect on the final appearance of the yarn. A yarn spun from thoroughly blended fiber will look more uniform than one spun from a casual blend. Fibers of contrasting value (lightness or darkness) will look mottled unless they are thoroughly blended. Conversely, fibers of similar value will produce a more homogeneous yarn, even if blending is incomplete.

Your procedures will be different if you want a uniformly blended yarn than if you want one with more variety. The blending process can actually start in the dyepot, or—with some colored fleeces—on the sheep's back.

Techniques for thorough blending

For evenly blended yarn, you will pay more attention at the teasing or picking stage. After you have chosen the colors and their proportions, begin to tease the fiber to be present in the smallest quantity along with the fiber of the next smallest quantity. When these two are blended, tease the combination with the color of the next smallest quantity, and so on. If you are using a wool picker, you may want to run the wool through several times.

Card the fiber once. Then separate each batt or rolag into several piles, combining each section with fiber from the other batts or rolags. Card each pile. Keep dividing and recarding until the mixture is as uniform as you want it to be. While you are spinning, keep an eye out for batts or rolags that are less homogeneous. Pull these aside and make sure they are interspersed randomly through the batch of yarn. It is possible to produce yarns so evenly blended that you have to look very carefully to see that they are composed of fibers of different colors, but it does take a lot of work.

Mottled and variegated effects

For a speckled or mottled look in the finished yarn, tease or pick as described above, but card the batts just once or twice before you spin. For another variation, pick the different colors separately and blend them as you card.

Special results can be created if you apply the fiber to the cards in a pattern. These will be more obvious if you use fibers with contrasting values. Different effects will be obtained from hand carders or a drum carder. Experiment with patterns of applying fibers to the cards or the drum.

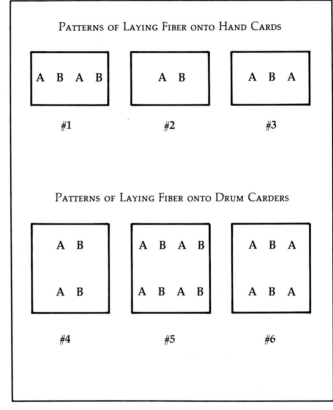

PATTERNS OF LAYING FIBER ONTO HAND CARDS

| A B A B | A B | A B A |
| #1 | #2 | #3 |

PATTERNS OF LAYING FIBER ONTO DRUM CARDERS

| A B / A B | A B A B / A B A B | A B A / A B A |
| #4 | #5 | #6 |

You can spin variegated yarn by alternating fiber colors, as shown in patterns 3 through 6. If you're using patterns 4 through 6, split the batt into three sections, dividing horizontally, roll each section into a "rolag," and spin from the end. The length of each color along the yarn will depend on the density of the rolag and on how fine your yarn is. Thin rolags spun into thick yarn will produce the most frequent color changes.

You can layer batts or rolags by adding different colors to the cards in succession. You can feed in waves of different colors. Or you can add a smidgeon of a different color after most of the carding has taken place, so the extra color occurs in just a thin layer.

The way in which you spin also influences your finished yarn. The striped batts in examples 4 through 6 above can be split lengthwise into strips, for a variegated yarn, or can be rolled lengthwise into a big rolag which you spin from its center, for a more randomly colored result.

Variations in spinning blends

With careful planning, you can create some truly wonderful yarns for special projects. Make ombré yarn by gradually changing the proportions of fiber colors, so each color melts into the next without a distinct transition. Make a monochromatic ombré by taking dyed fiber of one color and periodically adding white or black to it.

You can spin so each skein is slightly different from all the others, or you can shift colors frequently within every skein. Plan the color shifts with your finished project in mind.

Another possibility involves doing all the blending as you spin. Tease and card the colors separately and hold two rolags at once while you spin. The fibers can be drafted at the same time, half from each rolag; if the fibers contrast, the result will be a candy-striped effect. Subtler yarns result when you use fibers close in value. You can vary the proportions of each color as you spin or you can try to keep them constant.

A different type of variegated yarn results if you make rolags of different colors but change from one color to another in sequence as you spin. It is imperative that your joins are solid if you spin this type of yarn. Try spinning a yarn of mostly one color, with small amounts of a contrasting color added once in a while. Or change colors frequently, using many colors in random or controlled order. With very careful planning you can get ikat-like results when you weave with this type of yarn.

You can take your smooth blends even further. Everyone loves tweed yarns. They have a rich, earthy feeling. Often tweeds are made from heathered yarns sparked with *garnetted fibers*. Garnets are small nubs of fiber, felt, or slightly felted yarn which are added to the fiber supply during carding.

Tweeds

You'll need to experiment to know when is the best time to add the bits, and how much carding to do after they are added. Your choices will depend on whether you want the

nubs to look very distinct or to be more thoroughly incorporated into the yarn. They will also depend on how compact the nubs are when you start. Snippets of a loosely spun singles yarn will lose their distinct shape faster than bits of hard felt.

Garnetted nubs can be almost any color. A more exciting yarn will have nubs that contrast with the main yarn color. Lots of different colors of nubs in one tweed yarn look good.

The only drawback to spinning this type of yarn is that cutting all those little bits can get extremely tedious, and you may be hampered by the blisters which pop up on your scissors hand. Hold a bundle of yarns at once, so each snip nets a number of tidbits.

If you intend to make a project which involves more than one skein of yarn, you will need to keep track of your blending process. You'll need to record the proportions of each fiber used, as well as your preparation and spinning methods. It's easiest to keep track of amounts of fiber by weighing them. Write down information about how you teased or picked the fiber, how you applied it to the cards or the drum, the number of times it was carded, and the way you spun it. If you write down all these things and faithfully follow your notes, your yarn will not look like it came from a handful of different dyelots!

Your sample notebook will have even greater value if you incorporate examples of color blends. I strongly recommend that spinners take the time to make a series of color blending samples. This is a great project for study groups or guilds (each participant can spin enough of an assigned technique to provide samples for every other member). It only takes one hand-carded rolag to produce a mini-skein, although to make a good reference set you should use larger quantities of fiber and weigh them, so you can record exact proportions.

Cover the territory: value gradations in hues and neutrals, color wheels, blends including two colors, blends of three or more. Try to get brown without using any brown fiber. Dye two different sets of primaries (red, yellow, and blue; yellow, magenta, and turquoise) and see what differences show up.

Keeping track of blends

Blending games

TWEED YARNS. Garnetted fibers are added to a rose wool and angora base (left) and a purple and white angora base (center). At lower right, a similar multicolored effect occurred when linen was dyed for variegations, then plied with a commercial natural two-ply.

Once you have your color-blended yarn, there are even more possibilities. You can use these combinations in fancy plying techniques: spirals, bouclés, or simple two-ply yarns.

Fiber blending

Imagine a luscious blend of silk and angora. The possibilities are endless! You can combine fibers in two different ways, for different results. You can card them together, to create a blended singles, or you can join two strands of yarn — one silk and one angora — into a plied harmony.

There are lots of reasons to blend fibers. You can use up small quantities of fiber; you can "stretch" expensive fibers; or you can make a slippery or short fiber easier to spin. From the standpoint of yarn design, the most important reason to blend is that you can maximize the positive qualities or minimize the negatives in a particular fiber. You need to know enough about the various fibers to make informed decisions about blending.

Appropriate fiber blends

Here are a couple of examples of appropriate blends. Say you want to spin yarn for a fuzzy hat.

You consider combining silk top with Samoyed dog hair. Both fibers are soft and won't be itchy — a good sign. The yarn will derive luster and strength from the silk, and fluffiness from the dog hair. This looks like a good blend which will take positive attributes from both its fibers provided you cut the top into lengths about the same as the dog hair, so they will card together evenly.

You could produce a different blend for the same project. Mohair is a dense fiber which offers the potential for fuzziness, as well as strength and luster, but it is very heavy for use in garments. You have some wool which isn't very strong or interesting by itself but can add needed loft in a blend. By joining these fibers you would minimize the undesirable qualities in each.

When to blend?

Once you have decided which fibers to blend, you still need to think about whether to blend in the preparation stage or in spinning, and about how thoroughly mixed they should be. It's a good idea to experiment before you decide which method best suits your purpose. Blending in plying is straightforward. I'll go into more detail on the factors affecting carded blends.

In general, your blend will be more homogeneous if the staple lengths of the component fibers are similar. More heavily textured yarns can be obtained from fibers of different staple lengths, but be sure to add enough twist so the clumps of shorter fibers don't fall out.

When you are blending both fibers and colors, you may want to handpick or use a picker in a sequence which makes the blend more thorough. For instance, say you want to blend several colors of cotton and one color of silk noil. First blend the cotton: pick and scramble the colors together. Then take a clump of multicolored cotton and card it with the silk. This will make life simpler: you don't have to grab a snippet each of six colors of cotton and one handful of silk.

For consistency, weigh the overall quantities of each fiber which you intend to use in your finished blend. Place each type of fiber in a separate pile, and remove fiber from the piles in the same proportions. You should use up all the piles at the same time in the end.

Naturally, blending can be done on hand cards. Your drum carder will need fine card clothing to work well with fine fibers. If you don't have a drum carder with fine teeth, you can sometimes use the coarse drum for a rough initial blending. Then you can do a second carding with hand cards. This speeds up the process a great deal.

MAKING YARN

Fiber selection, preparation, and dyeing done, we're ready to actually make the yarn. Assuming you have done some basic spinning before, we can explore how to make more advanced forms of singles, plies, and fancy yarns.

First, though, you need access to one source of structural ideas — commercial yarns. And while you're in the yarn store, you may want to make note of what's there. You might find the perfect companion strand to use with your handspun, or some commercial yarns which could be turned into treasures by a trip or two through your spinning wheel.

Commercial yarns as inspiration

I get a tremendous amount of inspiration from studying the construction of commercial yarns. I find color and texture ideas. I discover ideas for new combinations. Many of the ideas in this book have been inspired by commercial yarns. Sometimes I buy complicated commercial novelty yarns just to pull them apart and see how they work.

Once in a while I try to imitate a commercial yarn in a handspun version, but my intent then is only to be sure I truly understand its structure and to improve my technical abilities. I want my handspun yarns to be unique, not something which is available in a store.

The Yarn Detective

I sometimes feel like a "yarn detective" as I carefully untwist and dissect a yarn under study. The following method will help you become a yarn analyst.

1. Look at a cut yarn end. Unply it a little, to see how many individual strands are included in the finished yarn.
2. Look at the color of each strand. Is any element space-dyed? If so, what was the color sequence?
3. Try to determine the fiber content of each strand. (The labels provide clues.)
4. How thick is each strand? How thoroughly is it twisted?
5. Think about how the yarns were plied together. How much twist was used? What tension? In what sequence were the strands joined?

Creating new yarns with commercial yarns

The use of commercial yarns in handspinning has had little exploration, but holds tremendous potential. Whether I use handspun or commercial yarn at any stage of the spinning process depends on the final look I want. If commercial yarns help me get to my destination, I certainly will use them. The industrial revolution happened for a reason and I want to use it to my advantage.

Combining commercial yarns with handspun

Sometimes I combine commercial yarns with handspun. I like to knit with plied yarns, to minimize the possibility of singles slant, so I often ply my singles with one or more commercial yarns. Another interesting combination results from plying a fine commercial novelty yarn with a plain handspun singles. Or a textured commercial cotton yarn could be nested in lightly corespun silk. You could make a knot yarn from fine, shiny, space-dyed silk and combine it with commercial brushed wool or mohair: the shiny knots will peek out of the fuzz. The possibilities are endless!

At other times I combine and recombine commercial yarns to make my own unusual composites. Several coordinated yarns can be made for a project from a base collection of commercial yarns. For example, you might weave a summer top from two-ply cotton. You can easily make accent yarns, such as bouclés and knots, from the same cotton supplemented with other commercial products. Yarns with different structures made from identical components, will always go well together. This is a great way to use up those old yarns which have been on your shelf too long! An additional benefit of making your own coordinating textured yarns is that you don't have to buy a full skein when you only need a few yards.

Texture with singles

You can make a textured yarn without plying. The several simple techniques for doing this include spinning from uncarded fiber, making a curly or "fuzzy" yarn, and producing intentional slubs. You can use these yarns as they are, or you can ply them to make fancier and more durable yarns.

We normally think of spinning as an orderly process of teasing, carding, spinning, and setting twist. By following a sequence of this sort, we get normal-looking handspun yarns. We can substitute combing for teasing-and-carding, but the product is still an ordinary, useful, possibly boring yarn. This routine can be short-circuited if we want to produce different and interesting results.

The options for fiber preparations include spinning from:
- unteased fiber
- teased but uncarded fiber
- roughly carded fiber
- fiber which has been carded several times

Color photo of textured singles on page 58.

The same fiber will yield quite different results, depending on its preparation. In general, the cruder preparations result in more heavily textured yarns.

Curly yarn

The texture of the curly, shiny locks of mohair and some of the wool breeds, such as Lincoln and Teeswater, is exquisite. With "normal" fiber preparation, this texture is obliterated. By spinning directly from these locks, we can preserve their identity in our yarn.

The resulting yarn makes a wonderful accent. It only takes a few shots to enliven a weaving. The yarn can be used for knitting, but remember that the outstanding texture will remain on the purl side of the fabric. If you use a lot of this yarn in a garment, it will—like the fibers which cause the effect—be heavy. This yarn would make a wonderful accent rug, although a corespun version (explained under plying) would be more durable.

I like to tease the raw fiber lightly, to open it up a little so drafting is easier. Matted fiber won't draft, so it doesn't work well.

To spin this yarn, use a wheel with a large orifice and big flyer hooks so the curly fibers won't get hung up. Draft carefully as you spin and try to keep the curly ends of the fiber as distinct as possible.

Avoid super-thin sections in the yarn, which will tend to break. Mohair is so slippery you need to be extremely attentive. If it doesn't have enough twist, it will fall apart. Test your yarn for strength by putting some tension on it.

If the yarn isn't holding together well, consider corespinning and using the curly, lightly teased fiber as the wrapping element. You'll also find corespinning useful when you want to make a thicker textured yarn.

Curly yarn is beautiful whether it's natural-colored, all one color, or space-dyed. You can blend colors by spinning from mixed colors of lightly teased fiber or by alternating different colors as you spin.

Fuzzy yarn

"Fuzzy yarn" is the handspun version of commercial brushed mohair or wool yarns. The yarn is fine and light, but seems both bulkier and softer than it really is. Knitters can create luxurious sweaters with it, but remember that a yarn cannot ultimately be any softer than the fiber used to create it. Kid mohair is a good choice for use next to the skin. Fabrics made with this yarn are soft and light, but will have a tendency to pill and are not suited for rugged use. It is a lovely yarn, but must be used appropriately.

The commercial variant consists of a fine core with a halo of fuzzy individual fibers sticking out in all directions. It is made from a sort of loopy bouclé. The loops are cut, or broken by severe brushing, and the loose fibers create the fluffy look. A nylon core or binder often gives these yarns strength.

How mills make fuzzy yarn

The handspun type of fuzzy yarn is a modified singles. There are basically two ways to make handspun fuzzies.

First, you can spin a conventional yarn and, as they do in spinning mills, brush it with your hand cards or a dog brush. This method has always seemed ruthless to me. In addition, it is slow, you will never be able to brush all sides of the yarn evenly, and you may seriously damage the yarn by snagging a big piece of fiber. A better approach would be to spin the same conventional yarn, to knit or weave it into its finished form (making a fairly open fabric), and then to brush the completed piece with a firm hairbrush or a dog brush. You would get a fuzzy surface, but the fabric structure would help keep the yarn intact during brushing.

Second, you can make the "fuzz" while you spin. Begin making a fine yarn with medium twist. While your right hand is drafting, gently use your left hand to pull some fibers from the drafting zone and toward the left. These fibers will become slightly disengaged from the yarn and will fluff out around it. The motion is one of gentle plucking. Be subtle or you will break the yarn. Repeat this motion throughout the spinning process, and try to keep the yarn's core fairly fine. After spinning, either steam or wash very gently to set the twist — agitation will produce felt.

A gentler way

Pluck as you spin

This technique works best with long animal fibers, such as wool or mohair. It's best to dye the fiber before you spin, since dyeing will tend to felt or mat the yarn. You can get some interesting variations through the color-blending techniques. Try spinning the yarn from rainbow batts, to make heathered or variegated yarn. Or spin with soft kid mohair or a mohair/silk blend for luxurious results.

Before you knit or weave with this yarn, you may want to ply it with another yarn to strengthen it and eliminate any tendency toward singles slant. Ply it loosely with a

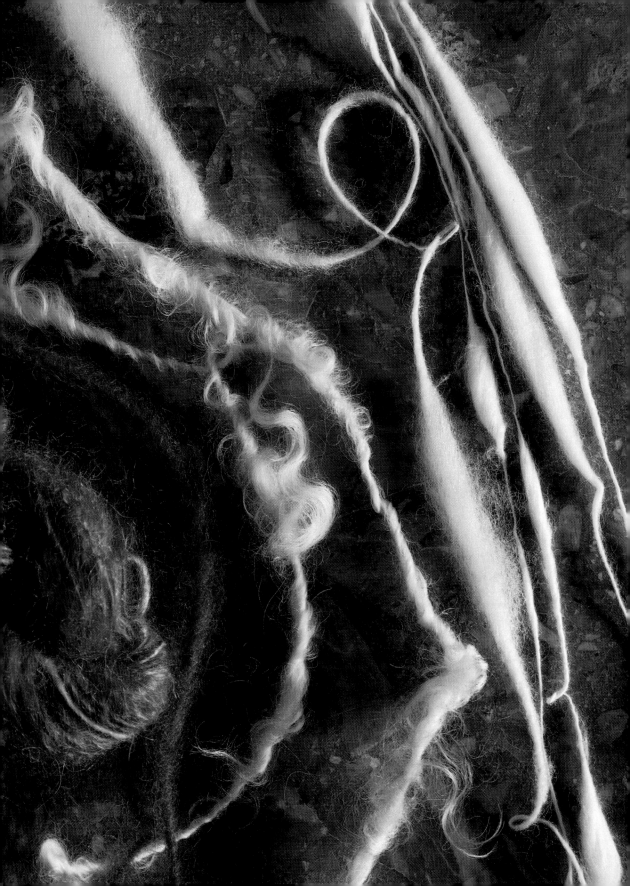

sewing-thread-weight yarn to keep its loftiness intact.

For weaving, use this yarn as weft, or set it very openly as warp. It can be too sticky and not strong enough for warp. The resulting fabric can be brushed with a hairbrush for more softness.

This yarn can also be combined with other yarns (handspun or commercial) to create unique novelty yarns. For example, you could ply it loosely with a knot yarn made of shiny silk: the knots will glisten through a veil of soft fiber. Use your imagination to think up wonderful new combinations.

Slub yarn

Slubs are thicker, less twisted areas in a basically thin, well-twisted singles yarn. It seems that when we are learning to spin we can only produce, to our dismay, slub yarns. We work hard to eliminate these beasts and to spin only smooth, even yarns. Sometimes when we achieve our goal we find ourselves yearning for that slubby old "beginners' yarn."

Slubs can be fun!

Often slubby yarns are equated with handspun. Spinning mills try to approximate handspun with thick-and-thin yarns. Careful inspection of these commercial yarns reveals that the slubs occur with amazing regularity, and that they are uniform in size. Handspun slub yarn is more interesting to look at and work with because its texture is more naturally random.

Slub yarns are wonderful to use in making fancy plied yarns. They are lovely in spiral yarns, especially in some of the locked spiral techniques.

Slub yarns can be used for knitting, crocheting, or weaving, although in weaving they should be used only as weft. The slubs tend to pill and abrade more than the adjacent, thinner areas of yarn, which is bad news in the reed and heddles. It also means your slub-yarn projects should not receive hard wear.

To make slub yarn, begin spinning as you would for normal singles yarn. Use a medium-length wool fiber for your first experiment. Draft normally with your right hand, then with that hand grasp the fiber in the triangle of the drafting zone — this fiber will become the slub; continue to draft

TEXTURED SINGLES. (1) Fuzzy yarn of kid mohair. (2) Slubs. (3) Curly yarn of mohair.

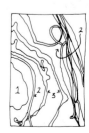

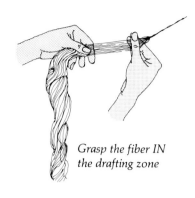

Grasp the fiber IN the drafting zone

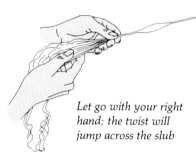

Let go with your right hand; the twist will jump across the slub

Variables in plying

Reasons to ply

behind the slub-to-be with your left hand. After you have drafted a small length, let go with your right hand. The twist will skip over the slub and enter the new drafting zone. Begin drafting with the right hand again.

The length of the slub is determined by the staple length of your fiber. Short fibers make short slubs, long fibers make long slubs. Try slub yarns in fibers of different lengths. Make a cotton slub.

The type of fiber preparation affects the slub's thickness. Slubs in yarns spun from carded rolags will be light and airy — and very subject to pilling. Slubs in yarn spun from commercial rovings tend to be more dense and durable. Experiment by working with batts from a drum carder. What is your yarn like if you divide the batt lengthwise and spin it in semi-worsted style? How about crosswise divisions and woolen style? Make a slub yarn from combed top. Beautiful slub yarn can be spun from fiber prepared using color-blending methods.

Plying techniques

Plying is the process of twisting two or more yarns together. It can take many forms and leads to a wide variety of smooth or textured yarns, such as bouclés, gimps, and ratinés. Plying generally produces a stronger yarn than a singles. Many variables within plying affect the final yarn, including:

> amount of twist
> direction of twist
> thickness and density of singles
> type of fiber in singles
> color

A "normal" *plying* routine involves twisting two singles yarns together in a direction opposite to that in which they were originally spun. Why would you want to ply? You have to spin twice as much or more to get yarn of a specific grist.

First, plying helps balance the twist in a yarn. This is especially important when you want to knit with your yarn. You can also rescue a "doomed" yarn which contains either too much or too little twist — plying can either add or subtract twist.

Second, certain textured yarns can only be made by plying. Spirals, bouclés, and knots fall in this category.

Third, some color techniques require plying. Ply a light and a dark yarn together and you'll get a marled yarn.

Making Yarn

Fourth, plying increases the strength and durability of a yarn. Since the thickness is doubled or tripled, the strength is, too. Since the fibers are more securely locked into place, plied yarns don't pill as much as singles.

Fifth, a plied yarn tends to be lighter in weight and warmer than a singles of similar yards per pound. There's more air space between the yarns and the twist opens out to trap more warmth.

Sixth, you can control your drafting better on a thin yarn. It is difficult to draft a thick mass of fiber to spin a thick yarn (your early spinning experience to the contrary), so you'll be able to guide the results better if you draft fine individual yarns and then ply them to the desired thickness.

I would be very surprised if you have been spinning for any length of time at all and have not made a basic plied yarn. However, on any plied yarn, even the simple two-ply, you should consider the amount of twist and the tension under which your plying occurs very carefully.

How much twist depends on how you want the yarn to look and how you intend to use it. The amount of twist in the singles should be determined through samples of the proposed finished yarn. Since plying removes twist from the individual yarns, your singles must have extra twist to compensate. Keep a sample of the singles wound around cardboard nearby for reference as you work. The angle of plying twist can be measured with a protractor or by untwisting an inch of yarn, just as twist is measured in singles.

Amount of twist in the singles

The basics

Basic plying requires that the tension be equal on each of the two yarns. Some fancier constructions, such as the spiral and bouclé, use different amounts of tension on the components.

For good control in plying, the individual yarns must run freely and consistently from their sources. Two common methods of handling the yarn are by putting the bobbins on a lazy kate or by winding balls on a ballwinder.

If you use a lazy kate, try to have the same amount of yarn on each bobbin. You can use the spinning bobbins, or the smaller bobbins used for boat shuttles if your yarn is fine. Try to have the same amount of yarn on each bobbin because the tension will increase as the amount of yarn decreases.

It is often useful to establish control over yarn tension, especially when high-twist yarns are involved. You can make

Controlling yarn tension

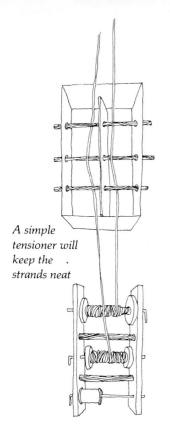

A simple tensioner will keep the strands neat

Plying multiple strands

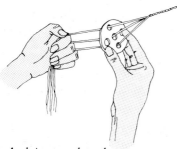

A plying template also maintains order

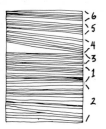

a tensioner with a series of dowels (or chopsticks) set into a shoe box to control the yarns' tension as the strands travel toward the spinning wheel. A cardboard divider can keep the individual yarns separate. You may need to add weight to the bottom of the box to keep it stationary. More elegant tensioning devices can be made using this basic idea.

If you're using balls, place them at your feet and pull the yarns out from the centers of the balls. If you have only one ball, or if you want to be sure both plying strands run out at the same time, you can use one strand from the center of the ball and one from the outside of the same ball. It's tricky to keep the two ends from tangling before they are twisted together; stick the index finger of one hand in the ball's center hole and use the other hand to tension the two yarns as they twist together.

There is a theory that you should always ply the "same ends" of yarn together. That is, the beginning (first-spun) end of one strand should be plied with the beginning end of another. I haven't found that this makes any difference.

Plying need not be limited to two strands, nor to one plying sequence. You can ply three or more singles together. Or you can make two or more two-ply yarns, and ply them together in the opposite direction. Because of the time required, I spin very few multi-ply yarns where all of the singles are identical. However, many people feel that the benefits reward the extra effort. Multi-plied yarns are lighter and warmer than singles or two-plies of similar grist. They may pill less.

I prefer to combine yarns of different fibers and colors when I ply. For example, I might use a fine commercial natural linen, a fine commercial cotton in a neutral color, and a slightly slubby space-dyed handspun silk. I enjoy plying combinations of shiny and dull yarns.

When you want to combine yarns of different fibers, consider the potential shrinkage of each yarn. If some yarns in a complex plied yarn shrink more than others, the yarns which don't shrink as much will form loose loops.

A *plying template* is a simple device: it's a disk with holes in it. The yarns feed through the holes on their way to be plied. This helps keep the singles organized and promotes even plying tension. A template is especially helpful when

BASIC PLYING. (1) Singles, (2) solid and two-color balanced plies. (3) Singles, (4) two Z singles, plied S, (5) two Z singles, plied Z (cable), (6) two singles, one Z and one S, plied Z.

Making Yarn

you are plying more than two strands at once. You can experiment with the plastic shaker lid from a spice bottle to see if you like using a template. More elegant versions of the tool are made of wood, and can be home-made or purchased.

For evenly plied yarn, count the number of times you treadle while the strands twist together for a fixed length of new yarn, let the finished yarn feed onto the bobbin, and then repeat this process. Alternatively, you can let the yarn feed continuously into the orifice and employ your fingers or a plying template to control the amount of twist which is allowed to enter the yarn. Stop periodically and measure the twists per inch or the angle of twist.

Plying can be *balanced* or *unbalanced*. To check the yarn for balance, if that's what you want, stop and let the yarn relax before it feeds onto the bobbin. If it doesn't twist back on itself, the plying is balanced. Unbalanced plying means there are significantly more or fewer twists per inch in the ply than in the component singles.

Navajo ply

The Navajo ply lets you make a three-ply yarn from one ball or bobbin of singles. It's a lot like crocheting a loopy chain with your fingers while the yarn is being twisted. You'll find it handy when you want to ply space-dyed or variegated yarn and keep the different colors fairly distinct. Like the no-loose-ends ball method of making a two-ply, this method lets all your strands end evenly.

This method is far easier to do than the directions may make it seem. Use a fine singles, since it will be tripled in the finished yarn. A smooth, even yarn is easier to pull through the loops than a textured strand.

Start with the slowest ratio on your wheel. Don't start treadling yet. Tie the singles yarn onto the leader. Make a slip knot, just as you would to start crocheting, with a loop approximately 6 to 8 inches in length. Hold the loop open with your right hand, using your thumb and as many fingers as are comfortable. Your left hand will tension the unplied yarn. Practice the hand motions before you start the wheel. Use your right forefinger as if it were a crochet hook and pull a second loop through the starting loop. Make the

Balanced and unbalanced plying

Reach through the loop

Pull the yarn through in another loop

PLYING. (1) Singles, (2) two-ply, (3) four-plies (3B has more twist since it will be made into an eight-ply), (4) eight-plies (different color arrangements in component four-ply yarns). (5) Hand-dyed commercial silk singles, (6) two-ply, (7) Navajo ply.

Making Yarn

new loop between 4 and 6 inches long and insert all of the same right-hand fingers you used on the previous loop. Repeat. When this feels good, start treadling in the direction opposite to that of the original spinning.

The size of the loops isn't critical. Make them whatever size feels comfortable. If you are using variegated yarn, you can make the loops different lengths to correspond to the changing colors of the yarn. Experiment with the location of your left hand. It is easier if your left hand is closer to the orifice as you pull the loop through.

Variations on Navajo plying

You need not limit yourself to a standard Navajo three-ply. Try a double Navajo ply: use a Navajo-plied yarn and do the Navajo ply again. This will produce a nine-stranded yarn. If you plan to do this, add extra twist when you do the first plying so the finished yarn will be more balanced. Double Navajo plying is a good way to use leftover fine commercial yarns.

Corespinning

This is a technique in which unspun fiber, rather than spun yarn, wraps around a core yarn. A dazzling variety of yarns can be created by varying the size, color, texture, and/or luster of the core yarn and the outer fiber.

Cores can be as thin as silk sewing thread or as thick as you please. A slender wrapping of gossamer silk will yield a delicate thread, while a deep layer of coarse mohair results in a bulky, lustrous yarn.

This technique is used commercially to create novelty yarns for every purpose, from rug weaving to knitting. You can detect the corespun origins of a commercial yarn by examining a cut end for both core and wrapping layers.

Corespinning can save time and money

One of the best things about corespinning is that the core can be almost any yarn or combination of yarns. This means the spinner can transform the most hideous yarn into an inspiring beauty. For the ultimate transformation, cover a repulsive core yarn completely . . . only you will know that the luscious, rainbow-dyed wrapper is hiding something. You can even convert fine yarns into a bulky yarn by using several thin strands together as one core. Unloved fiber can sometimes find a useful life as a single-ply core.

Expensive fibers or those in limited supply can be conserved through corespinning. Why use a valuable fiber for the center of a yarn when it won't be visible anyway? Beautiful corespun bulky yarns can build their foundations around economical mill-ends, with your special stash of high-quality wool on the surface.

Because you don't have to spin all the fiber you need to create an original yarn, corespinning can also save you time. By purchasing commercial core yarns, you preserve your own time for attention to the visible, outer layer.

The added strength the core gives to these yarns is a big advantage under certain circumstances. For example, although low-twist, fluffy yarns are appealing, they are also weak and tend to self-destruct readily. With corespinning you can create a strong yarn that looks lighter than air. Also, singles like the curly yarn already described offer exciting texture but are prone to slipping apart in their thin spots. A strong core will prevent this wonderful yarn from disintegrating when your application requires it to have backbone.

Corespinning allows you to more easily spin thick, strong, compact yarns. More spinning control is possible when you're drafting fiber for a bulky corespun than for a bulky singles. You can make this yarn stiffer than would be possible in a singles, by using a compact core yarn and keeping high tension on the wrapping fiber.

The distinctive structure of corespun yarns suggests some exciting design possibilities. When you plan your yarn, you can consider the size, color, and texture of the core, as well as the color, texture, and coverage of the wrapping fiber. Think about the yarn's intended purpose and the characteristics you'd like it to have.

Design in corespinning

How much the core yarn's appearance matters will depend on whether it will be visible in the finished yarn. If the core color isn't quite right, no problem . . . just wrap it with a thin layer of natural or dyed fiber, to tone down, lighten, or brighten it. Multiple fine core yarns of different colors covered with a thin wrapping layer can be nice. An example of effective use of color in a core yarn comes from a tweed core with a variety of colorful nubs that peek out through a thin haze of wrapping fiber.

The density and thoroughness of the wrapping fiber's coverage become important elements in the design of this type of yarn. If a thin layer is used, the core will show; thick layers will completely obscure it. A thin layer of a wrapping fiber can be used as a binder to hold several core yarns together.

To select the core yarn, consider the look you want for the yarn and its ultimate use. If the core will be completely covered, you can use a core yarn color that blends with the wrapping fiber — or you can select something which doesn't and make sure it's always completely hidden. If you plan to weave a rug, the core should be compact and have medium to high twist. For knitting or weaving garments, a more loosely spun or finer core yarn is appropriate. You'll find that most wrapping fibers stick to a fuzzy core yarn better than to a smooth one. Unusual corespun yarns can be made from textured yarns. For example, you can retain the texture of a cotton novelty yarn by wrapping it with a thin, tight layer of silk top.

The thickness of the core yarn(s) largely determines the diameter of the finished corespun yarn, but the wrapping fiber is typically its focal point. The staple length of the wrapping fiber should be enough to wrap at least twice around the core, so the fibers will be well secured. Wool, silk, and mohair are dependable wrapping fibers because they're long enough.

Color-blending techniques — such as heathering, garnetting, and so forth — create exceptionally beautiful yarns through this technique. Rainbow-dyed fibers can be shown off well in corespun structures. Try syringe-dyed silk top as a wrapping fiber. Different colors or blends of wrapping fibers can be changed at intervals to give a space-dyed look to the finished yarn. For an interesting rug, try subtle color gradations in hue, value, and intensity.

Choose the texture of the wrapping fiber with care, to make sure you get the results you want. As always, parallel and consistent fiber preparations lead to smooth, even yarns. Coarse wool wrapping fiber will produce a very different yarn than will smooth, lustrous, combed silk top. Which one is better? That depends on your intended use of the yarn. Ultra-textured corespun yarns feature wrapping fiber of teased mohair or curly wools. Try other fiber combinations, such as silk noil and wool.

Before you start, be sure to set your wheel at its lowest drive ratio so your hands will have plenty of time to work. Beginners should first try a medium-weight core yarn, such as a commercial two-ply. To prevent overtwist, spin the core yarn in the opposite direction to that in which it was originally spun (singles) or plied.

The spinning technique consists of drafting out to the side while the drafted fiber wraps around the core. To start, tie the core yarn(s) onto the bobbin leader. Set the tension on

Corespinning technique

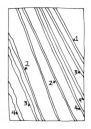

CREPE YARNS. Two series of crepes. (1) Singles, (2) two-plies on their way to being crepes, (3) three-ply crepes, (4) four-ply crepes.

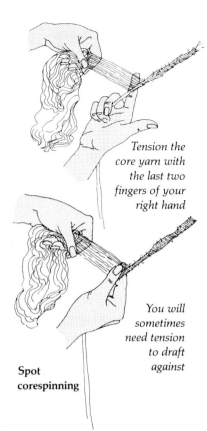

Tension the core yarn with the last two fingers of your right hand

You will sometimes need tension to draft against

Spot corespinning

the wheel so there is a little pull. The core yarn should feed freely through your right hand, and the drafting fiber is held loosely to the left. The left hand holds the wrapping fiber near the drafting zone. Use the last two fingers of the right hand to hold the core yarn taut. The thumb and first finger of the right hand should be available to grasp the drafted fiber at times, to provide tension to draft against.

To attach the wrapping fiber, simply lay the fibers on the core yarn while treadling. They will either become attached to the core or stick to other wrapping fibers covering the yarn. Draft to the left, then allow the fiber to wrap around the core. After a while, you will be able to draft and wrap at the same time instead of alternating the two actions.

The tension used when wrapping fiber around the core determines whether a tight, stiff yarn or a softer, fluffier one is spun. The tension is controlled by the thumb and first finger of your right hand. Increased pressure by these fingers on the drafted fiber while it wraps around the core results in a tighter yarn. Loose tension creates a halo effect of fluffy fiber around the core. After spinning, set the twist with steam or water.

Spot corespinning is a variation where bare core alternates with wrapped core. You can use it to add limited areas of a different color or texture, or to build up bumps.

Begin as for regular corespinning, but pull the wrapping fiber source away to the left after some fiber has wrapped. Allow the bare core to advance, and start wrapping again whenever you want. Continue alternating bare core with wrapped spots. For small areas of corespinning, separate the wrapping fiber into small clumps which contain just enough fiber for each spot. For textured spots, try a dog hair wrapper; you may need to ply the yarn after corespinning to secure the dog hair fully. If you build up thick layers of wrapping fiber in limited areas, the bumps resemble the knots in a knot yarn.

My favorite use for corespun yarn is as an accent in weaving. Bold texture and exciting color effects can be easily produced. To emphasize the texture, bring the yarn to the surface of a predominantly plain weave fabric by working from a straight twill threading and raising only one shaft for the picks of corespun yarn: the textured yarn will be held down by only every fourth warp. I also use thick corespun as an accent warp; your reed will have to be coarse enough to handle it. I've been known to cut a reed to make extra-wide dents to accommodate it. If it's really bulky, you may also need to make a custom-tied string heddle for it. To attach a

Making Yarn

thick corespun warp to the front or back apron bar, attach a thinner yarn to its end and then tie this extension to the apron bar.

You can also use corespun as an accent yarn by couching it onto woven or knitted fabric after the cloth has been washed and/or fulled. I add the corespun at this stage because it tends to shrink less than other yarns and the fabric remains flatter if I wait. You can add corespun stripes, or exercise a freer approach and make gracefully curved lines. It's best to use this application in areas of a garment which won't need to endure a lot of abrasion.

Strong rugs which are quick to weave are ideal projects for using corespun yarn. For maximum durability, use a long-fibered wool or mohair with medium to tight tension. Be sure to use a strong, compact core yarn.

Finer corespun can be used for knitting, crocheting, or weaving as a primary yarn, as opposed to an accent. For flexible yarns, use a fine core and wrap with medium to loose tension.

Corespun also works well in basket making. Use it as a visible core in coiled baskets, or crochet it with a large hook.

Spiral yarns

The elegance and simplicity of spiral yarns make them favorites. They are constructed through a plying technique where a "wrapping" yarn spirals like a corkscrew around a finer core yarn. Spiral yarns are not only beautiful and useful by themselves, but can also be used to create more complicated yarns, such as gimps and bouclés.

Spiral yarns are a first-rate choice for accent wefts in weaving. They are striking when used as an occasional weft in a web composed primarily of less-textured yarns, particularly if the spiral's color contrasts with that of its background. Spiral yarns are difficult as warp, and they are less successful as knitting yarns. If you use them for knitting, they'll add subtle texture to the purl side of your fabric.

Since the wrapping yarn is the focal point, I make sure that it is the most interesting fiber element. You can use a slub, color-blended, fiber-blended, or space-dyed yarn as a wrapper. Two singles wrapped at the same time can completely encase the core.

The wrapping yarn should be significantly thicker than the core yarn. The twist can vary. A loosely twisted wrapping yarn will give you a fluffy appearance, and a tightly twisted one will result in maximum durability. For loosely twisted wrapping yarns, longer fibers, such as Romney

Spiral yarns can be used as is, or form the basis for more complicated yarns

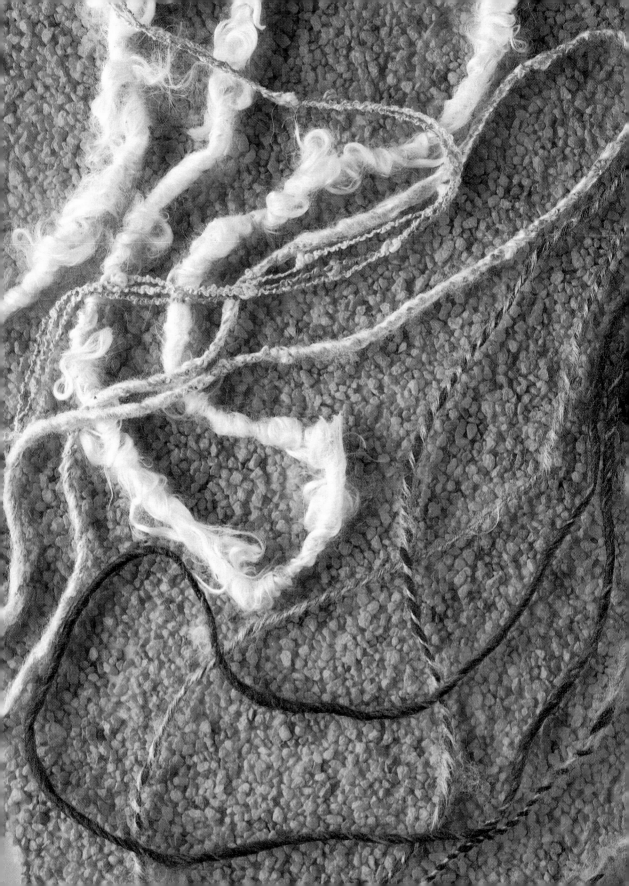

wool or silk, work well. The longer fibers help keep the wrapping yarn from disintegrating. If you want color in a fluffy wrapping yarn, dye the fibers before you spin them. Yarn tends to felt slightly in a hot dyebath, and will lose some of its loftiness if colored at that stage.

The core yarn should be carefully selected. Where the wrapping yarn carries the visual weight of this structure, you'll find that a "bashful" type of core yarn is often most effective. The core yarn should be strong, finer than the wrapping yarn, and harmonious with the overall design. I always use commercially spun yarns for the core. Sewing thread can be used for a very fine spiral yarn. The wrapping yarn will adhere best to a slightly hairy core yarn and may slide around on a slippery core.

I once spun a spiral yarn which was to have been the ultimate in spinning luxury. It consisted of a silk core with a cashmere wrapper. While the yarn looks wonderful and is fun to fondle, it is good for little else. The design is poor. The strong part (silk) is hidden in the core; the soft, short cashmere fibers on the outside are easily abraded. It could be used in a special evening garment that won't be used often, or I could add more twist to it, or I could ply it with something else to make it more durable.

When you want to make a spiral yarn, be sure to use a wheel whose hooks and orifice are large enough that the spirals will not get hung up as they feed onto the bobbin. If you have a choice, use a wrapping yarn that was spun in the same direction that the core yarn was spun or plied. In this case, you will make the spiral by plying in the opposite direction. If your core was spun or plied in a direction opposite to that of the wrapping yarn's twist, you will make the spiral by using the direction opposite to the wrapping yarn's twist. In both cases, it's most important to slightly *loosen* the wrapping yarn as you make the spiral.

Tie the core yarn onto the bobbin leader. Hold the core yarn taut with your right hand. Let the wrapping yarn wind loosely around the core yarn and allow the completed spiral yarn to feed onto the bobbin at a comfortable rate. Experiment with the angle at which you hold the wrapping yarn — a shallow angle will produce a subtler texture, while the

Spiral technique

Let the wrapping yarn coil loosely around the core

CORESPUN YARNS. (1) Heavy layer of mohair around three strands of commercial wool singles. (2) Three commercial cotton bouclés; the same wrapped with silk top. (3) Light corespinning over variegated handspun singles and (4) over three finer commercial yarns.

texture intensifies as the angle moves toward 90 degrees. You can also affect the yarn's texture through the tension with which you hold the wrapping yarn. The more loosely you control it, the more textured your yarn will be.

Bouclé yarns

Color photo of bouclés on page 76.

Bouclés, with their looped and crimped texture, are among the most exciting yarns to spin. Do you believe you can do this yourself? Absolutely!

Bouclé is a general term which refers to yarns which look loopy or curly. They are created with a structure called *locked spiral*. Some other names of yarns made with the locked spiral structure include gimp, loop, ratiné, and curled loop.

The locked spiral

These yarns are composed of a thicker wrapping, or "effect," yarn which is plied with a finer core, as we've seen before. But the two-ply yarn (a spiral — you recognized it) is then plied again with another fine *binder* yarn. The variations on this single basic structure are limitless. You can vary the wrapping yarn thickness (slubby yarns work well), amount of twist, fiber type, color of core and binder yarns, and so forth, to come up with a steady stream of unique and wonderful skeins.

Small amounts of bouclé yarns are effective as weaving accents in contrast to a plainer background. Appropriate uses include knitting, weaving, and crochet. Larger textured areas of bouclés are also beautiful.

Since some handspun bouclé yarns are too heavy for knitting, try alternating rows of bouclé with rows of a less-textured yarn, to reduce the weight of the knitted fabric. This also conserves the more time-consuming bouclé, although if you use commercial cores and binders this won't be a major factor. You can machine knit with bouclé on a bulky machine. If you have difficulty getting the yarn to feed smoothly, try the weaving-in technique of machine knitting.

Bouclés consist of three elements

Since bouclé yarns consist of three elements — the wrapper, the core, and the binder — you need to watch the thickness of each strand. The combination must be able to fit through the orifice of your wheel and not catch on the hooks. The wrapping yarn should be at least twice as thick as the core and binder yarns.

Bouclé technique

The first step in making a basic bouclé is to spin a spiral yarn. Hold the core yarn taut and allow the thicker wrapping yarn to spiral around it. The yarn should be plied in the opposite direction to the twist in the wrapping yarn. Let the wrapper wind loosely around the core — the more loosely it

Making Yarn

goes on, the loopier and more textured the finished yarn will be.

The binder yarn will stabilize the bouclé and prevent its loops from slipping along the core. Ply the spiral with a fine binder, working in the direction opposite to that of the first plying. Allow the spiral to wrap loosely around the binder. Your new yarn should look sort of like rickrack.

After you have tried the basic technique, you are ready for some of the exciting variations. This is not a complete compilation of the possibilities, but a starting place for you to begin your explorations of this wonderful structure.

For a more textured yarn, try the *push method*. While you perform the first plying, periodically push the wrapping yarn toward the orifice, so it completely covers the core from time to time. This produces a much loopier bouclé when you ply it with the binder. You can make a yarn which is consistently loopier, or one which has areas of dense and areas of "normal" loops, depending on how frequently you push.

A *double wrapping yarn* uses two wrapping strands simultaneously. This makes a much fuller bouclé. Hold both wrapping yarns in one hand and allow them to twist around the core. They may also twist around each other, but that's okay. Wrap so the core is completely covered. Then take that three-element yarn and ply it with a binder, as before.

You can use a two-ply wrapper instead of two singles, but the yarn looks different. Try making a yarn which has two wrappers of the same color, or one with two wrappers of different colors.

A *bump yarn* plays with the idea that the fiber type and preparation make a huge difference in the yarn's finished appearance. Spin a wrapping yarn from medium-to-fine wool top. Use a medium twist and let it have some thick and thin areas. When you ply this with the core yarn, push up frequently so the core is covered by the wrapper. When you combine this two-ply with the binder, ply them evenly so the two-ply doesn't wrap around the binder yarn, but they wrap around each other.

You can make a *silk gimp yarn*! It will be gorgeous! Spin a high-twist silk singles wrapping yarn; the extra twist is necessary so the final yarn will be strong and will resist pilling. If you succumb to the temptation of making a fluffy silk bouclé, you'll end up with an exquisite yarn which will pill a lot and not be lovely for long.

Make a spiral by plying the silk wrapper with a core. In the final plying, let the spiral wrap around the binder.

The binder stabilizes the yarn

Push the wrapping yarn toward the orifice from time to time

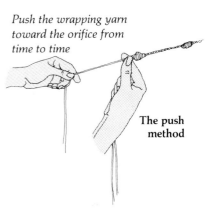

The push method

A double wrapping yarn

A bump yarn

A silk gimp

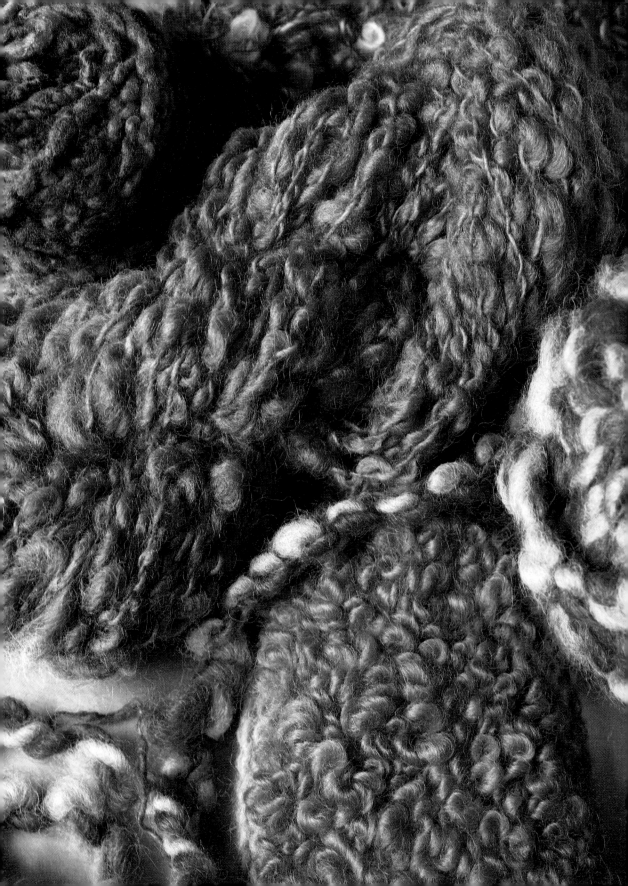

Loopy bouclé perplexed me for a long time. I kept trying and trying to produce one, and made some beautiful yarns, but a strand with distinct loops continued to elude me. One day I tried commercially prepared mohair top. The long-awaited loops magically appeared! The stiffness of the mohair top was the missing key. (Carded preparations of long-staple lustrous wool and mohair make yarns with fluffy loops.)

Spin a wrapping yarn with the mohair top, using medium twist. While you are spinning, check for the proper amount of twist by occasionally stopping and letting the yarn relax toward the orifice. You want loops—not kinks—to form. Ply the wrapping yarn with sewing-thread core. Allow several plying twists to form and then push the wrapping yarn up the core. A loop will form with each push. Then ply this yarn with a sewing-thread binder.

A *snarl yarn* uses a super-overtwisted wrapping yarn. Spin the wrapper so you can see overtwisted kinks in the singles. The wrapping yarn should be medium to fine in weight and evenly spun. Thick-and-thin yarn is difficult to work with, because the twist is irregularly distributed through the yarn.

Ply this wrapping yarn with a finer core yarn, but in the *same* direction as its original twist. To form a "snarl," allow a small section of wrapping yarn to pull up and relax, so it plies back on itself between your fingers and the area where it is plying with the core. Hold this self-plied section of the wrapping yarn so it wraps around the core. Repeat wherever you want a snarl. Ply this with a binder, using twist opposite to that of the wrapping yarn to remove some of the excess twist.

For ultra-snarly yarn, ply two snarl yarns together. . . .

What I call *jerky yarn* depends on a different kind of hand motion during the plying of the wrapper and the core. A fine to medium wrapping yarn seems to work best. Hold the wrapping yarn in your right hand and allow it to wrap around a core yarn. Occasionally jerk your right hand back and forth along the axis of the core yarn.

Experiment with plying in the same direction as the wrapping yarn twist, or in the opposite direction. See what hap-

Loopy bouclé

A snarl yarn

Color photo of snarl yarns on page 80.

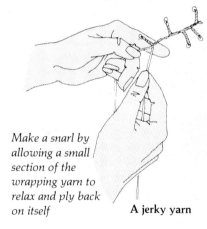

Make a snarl by allowing a small section of the wrapping yarn to relax and ply back on itself

A jerky yarn

BOUCLÉS AND LOOPY BOUCLÉS. The primary element in the ball at top left is wool top dyed before it was spun. At lower right is a loopy bouclé from carded wool. The binders in the center skein and the bicolor skein were handspun.

pens when the wrapping yarn is loosely twisted. And what if it's tightly twisted?

Knot yarns

Knot or seed or knop yarns are fancy yarns in which firm nubs alternate with normal plying. The nubs occur when you allow one yarn to wrap around the other in one area until a bump builds up. Knot yarns can be made of almost any fiber, and are gorgeous when knitted or woven.

Many textured yarns are beautiful, but not as long-wearing as we might like. The durability of knot yarn is unusual. If spun from hard-twisted components it will pill very little and will retain its beauty for a long time.

Knot yarn has tremendous design possibilities. By spinning it yourself, you can create the perfect yarn for your project. You can have just the right size of knots, the right spacing, and the right colors. Try making a knot yarn with a combination of shiny silk and matte cotton.

Other exciting effects result when you use space-dyed yarn, so multicolored knots occur. Experiment with a space-dyed yarn which has sections of contrasting value. For example, make two skeins that are mostly dark blue with one section of white. Ply them together and make knots only when white appears. When you knit or weave this yarn, the white knots will be in striking contrast to their background.

You can transform lackluster commercial singles or plied yarns into dazzling knot yarns. By using commercial yarns you save time and money and still create gorgeous, unique yarn. Try plying two knot yarns together for a super-knot yarn.

The same knot yarn will look quite different knitted than it does woven. Space your knots with your end use in mind. They'll be closer together for knitting than for weaving.

In knitting, most of the knots — as usual for textures — show up on the purl side. Plan your stitch accordingly. You can "stretch" the knot yarn by alternating it with rows of a related simpler yarn, or by using it only for certain areas of a garment, such as the top of the bodice or the sleeves.

In weaving, use knot yarn only as weft. Try a pick of it after several picks of a plainer yarn. To bring the knot yarn to the surface and emphasize it, thread to a straight twill and raise only one shaft when you use the knot yarn, so it will be tied down with only every fourth warp.

Careful selection of plying yarns will produce good knot yarn. You'll need firmly twisted components, because a lot

Knot yarn is unusually durable

Making Yarn

of twist is removed as the knot yarn is produced. Use yarns with sizes appropriate to the ultimate yarn.

Begin by attaching two plying yarns to the bobbin leader. Start to ply. To make a knot, hold one of the yarns taut — this will be the core yarn for the knot. Allow the other yarn to wrap back and forth around the core in one area, until the knot is the desired size. Continue plying normally. Alternate knots with normal plying.

Since strong twist can build up in the knot yarn, you should alternate knot-forming yarns. Ply normally, then form a knot with the right-hand strand; ply normally, and form a knot with the left-hand strand.

If you decide that your completed knot yarn contains too much twist, ply it in the reverse direction with a fine yarn (such as sewing thread). To maintain the original appearance of the yarn, select sewing thread in a closely related color. To change the look of the yarn, you can use a heavier yarn in a contrasting color.

Experiment with small and large knots, long and short knots, and the spacing of the knots. Try silk, cotton, linen, and wool. When you find a combination you like, make enough to knit or weave a sample fabric.

Tufted yarns

Sometimes known as nep, knop, or cage yarns, tufted yarns are created in the plying process. You intermittently insert small fiber clumps between the plying strands. Each clump gets wedged in to form a distinct bump in the yarn. The yarn's character is influenced by the color, luster, fiber type, and fiber length of the insertion. For maximum impact, I prefer fiber clumps which contrast in color, luster, or fuzziness to the plied yarns. You could use bits of soft dog hair, silk noil, carded fleece, or locks of wool or mohair. Try different colors of fiber, randomly placed along a two-ply yarn.

This yarn is quite textured and makes a gorgeous knitting yarn. If you want to, you can pull the clumps to the knit side of a stockinette fabric with a crochet hook after a piece has been knitted. The yarn can also be used for weaving or crochet.

You can tuft yarn any time you are plying. The base yarn can have two or more plies. I don't recommend using the Navajo plying technique, because the clusters cannot be adequately secured.

Before you begin your adventure with tufted yarn, pre-

Knot yarn technique

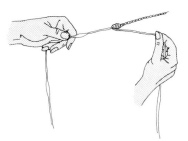

Hold one strand taut and let the other wrap back and forth in one area

Color photo of tufted yarns on page 82.

pare the fiber clumps and lay them where you can conveniently reach them. Even little clumps are effective. Start small so your orifice won't get clogged. If the fiber you plan to use is long, you can use scissors to cut the clumps — or use the long-fiber variation mentioned below.

Begin spinning as for regular plying. Ply for at least 6 inches, then insert a fiber clump between the yarns being plied. Allow the yarns to ply after the clump, to hold it in place. Repeat at will. The amount of twist in the plied yarns is important. It's important to anchor the fiber clumps securely: you'll be disappointed if they fall out of the finished fabric! Test some finished yarn by trying to pull the clumps out.

If you have long fibers and don't want to cut them, try using elongated clumps. Place them lengthwise along the axis of one of the plying yarns. Ply the yarns together; the fiber clump will be locked into place with several twists. When you knit or weave with this yarn the clump will be further secured.

You can use compact balls of fiber for clumps. You can felt the fiber and then cut it with scissors, or take a small amount of fiber, moisten it, and roll it between your palms.

The variation known as a *cage yarn* fastens the clumps in more firmly. I highly recommend this variation for its structural integrity.

While you are plying, insert a clump. Then let one of the singles yarns wrap back and forth around the cluster and the other singles. This motion is similar to the one used to make knot yarns. You'll make a knot with a few wraps right around the cluster.

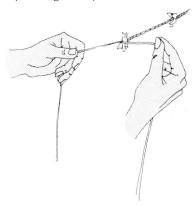

Secure the clumps by letting one of the singles wrap back over them

A cage yarn

Crepe yarns

Crepe yarns are quite different from crepe fabric. The fabric is created by weaving with highly twisted singles yarns. The yarn is a plying variation.

Three or more plies are used for crepe yarns, which are durable. Thicker versions can be used for purse straps, as decorative "braid" on fabric, or for button loops. Thinner versions can be used in the same ways as standard plied yarns.

Crepe yarns involve three or more strands

SNARL YARNS. (1) Singles, thread, and the snarl yarn made from them. (2) Snarl yarn made with fiber blended in carding. (3) Snarl yarn made with less twist in the singles.

To make a three-strand crepe yarn, begin by spinning one medium-twist S yarn and two medium-twist Z yarns. Since the finished yarn will be more than three times as thick as these component strands, make your singles accordingly fine. You will put *extra twist* in all spinning operations except the final plying.

Ply the two Z yarns in the S direction.

Ply the two-ply yarn with the S yarn in the Z direction.

You can achieve interesting effects by using different colors for each of the singles, and you can make crepe yarns with more than three plies.

Start with a three-ply, and then ply it with another singles which has been spun in the same direction as the last plying. For example, to continue with the three-strand crepe shown above, you would add another Z single and ply in the S direction.

A *cord*, *braid*, or *cable* is less round in cross-section than a crepe. It is made by plying together two yarns, each of which has two or more plies.

A cord, braid, or cable

To make a four-strand cord, spin four medium-twist Z singles. Make two two-ply yarns, spinning in the S direction. Then ply the two two-ply yarns together in the Z direction.

Elegant additions

Feathers: what an exotic material . . . what fun to play with! You may have seen gorgeous feather yarns in your local yarn shop and wondered how they were made. There are two approaches you can use to incorporate feathers in your handspun.

Feathers

The first consists of locking the feather shafts (their bases) through a yarn as it is being plied. This makes a yarn with secure feathers. It would be rather embarrassing, after all, to go to an elegant gathering in your exotic sweater and to leave a path of feathers behind.

The second is a variation of fiber blending. The feathers are cut up and then carded with other fibers.

Let's start with the plied method. These yarns are best used as accent yarns, in both knitting and weaving.

TUFTED YARNS. Tufts made from (1) snipped yarn, (2) Samoyed doghair, (3) wool, (4) mohair curls, and (5) elongated pieces of silk noil.

In knitting, the feathers will tend to stay on the purl side (where have you heard that before?) Plan the spacing of feathers in the yarn so you'll have them as often as you want them in the finished fabric.

For weaving, this yarn should—not surprisingly—be used only for weft. You will probably want to bring the feathers to the surface of the fabric as you lay in each pick, by pulling them up through the adjacent warps. You may want to alternate simpler yarns between shots of feather yarn, depending on the feather density you want.

To make this kind of yarn you need two fairly fine yarns, which you will ply together. The original strands can be singles or plied, handspun or commercial. They should be plied or spun in the same direction. The other essential element is feathers. Finding feathers was the problematic part for me, after I first figured out the technique by analyzing a commercial sample.

Where do you get feathers on a Sunday evening when you are in a feather craze? Well, I managed to find a feather duster in a nearby store. I pulled out some of the feathers, knowing the only use this feather duster would get would be in feather yarn. It certainly would never see any dusting action in my house.

Other, nonemergency, sources of feathers include craft and hobby shops, mail order suppliers, and friends who raise birds. Who knows, maybe your spinning will lead to yet another activity—aviculture.

Feathers are made mostly of protein and can be dyed with the same dyes used for wool and silk. I recently found another duster with all of its feathers in different colors—what fun! If your feathers seem too long, consider cutting them into smaller lengths.

You also need a wheel with a large orifice and big hooks. Use a slow wheel ratio setting while you get yourself going.

Have your feathers separated and within easy reach. Take the two yarns you plan to ply together and tie them onto the leader. Ply the yarns in the opposite direction to that in which they were spun or plied. Begin to ply them with a firm twist. Grasp a feather with its shaft facing away from you. Align it with one of the yarns (A), then allow the other yarn (B) to ply around both the feather shaft and yarn A. Let yarn B wrap at least three times to secure the feather shaft adequately.

Continue plying normally, and insert another feather when you want to. After you've secured a few feathers, stop

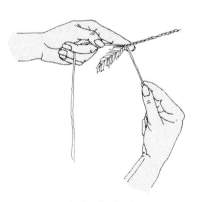

Insert the shaft of a feather between two plying strands

and test their sturdiness by trying gently to pull them out. If they end up in your hand instead of the yarn, you need to make more wraps or tighter ones. Try again; test again.

This yarn tends to be highly twisted when you are finished. Set the twist by steaming or wetting the yarn, but test the feathers with this treatment before you subject the yarn to it. Some feathers lose their fluffy look. If the yarn still seems to have too much twist, you can ply it with another fine yarn, or run it through the wheel by itself in the opposite direction to remove some twist. Or, for super-feather yarn, ply together two feathered yarns.

Variations abound. Alternate different colors or types of feathers. Change the color and thickness of the plying yarns. Play with spacing. Put two feathers in at once (try three if you're feeling dextrous). Let the wrapping yarn wind around just the feather's shaft or all the way to its tip. (You can apply the feather technique to cut pieces of yarn and make *shaggy yarn.*)

Shaggy yarn

One drawback to using feather yarns in garments is that the shafts are stiff and can be worse than a rug-quality wool against the skin. Sample for wearability with the swatch method described earlier. If your sample fails the test and you're determined to proceed regardless, you can line the section of the garment which contains feathers, or you can plan to wear a defensive undergarment.

The other method of making feather yarns involves blending the feathers with fiber during carding. My experience with this involved peacock feathers which were given to me after the long iridescent parts had been stripped from the main shaft. I got the fun colors, but in an unusual form. Each mini-feather had a fine shaft which wasn't very stiff. I cut the featherlets into smaller lengths and carded them with silk. When I spun this mixture, the iridescent feather parts created a lovely contrast to the base fiber.

You can add **beads, sequins, and seashells** to yarn by stringing them onto one yarn and then plying it with a second, plain yarn. You'll get a two-ply with intermittent treasures. This can be left as is, or plied again. It's well-suited for knitting or as a weft yarn. If you use small beads, this yarn can even go through a knitting machine.

Beads, sequins, and seashells

Color photo of beads, sequins, and metallics on page 90.

To make beaded yarn, first use a fine needle to thread the beads onto sewing thread which is still attached to the spool. Then remove the needle and put the thread spool on a lazy kate. This thread with beads will be yarn A. Tie both A and

its plain partner, B, to the bobbin leader. Begin plying the two yarns together, holding yarn A in your right hand and yarn B in your left. Try to keep a number of beads near your right hand and control their release with your right thumb and forefinger. Every once in a while, allow one of the beads to slide into the area where the yarns are plying and let it be twisted into place. Plan the density of the beads by your intended use and the density of beads you want in the finished fabric. If all the beads seem to slide to the floor, you may need to hold the beaded section of thread higher in the air so they stay closer to your right hand. Play with bead yarn as a component in a more complex yarn.

To use sequins, buy curved sequins or flat paillettes which already have holes in them. Thread them as you did the beads. If you use curved sequins, it will be easier to separate them later if you alternate the directions in which you thread them, so they don't nestle in together. For shells, you'll have to drill small holes with a fine bit before you can string them. Then proceed as described above.

You can play with the color of the beads or sequins, or use both together. You can alter the thickness, fiber, and color of your plying yarns. Or you can vary the frequency with which you insert the beads, sequins, or shells.

The use of **rags and ribbons** in knitting has been in vogue, and then out again. It comes and goes.

Rags and ribbons

Knitting with rags is a wonderful way to recycle fabrics and to create wonderful new knitting yarns. "Yarn" is made by cutting fabric into narrow strips. This is then knitted. Weavers have known this trick for years—rag rugs and other textiles are standard fare.

So far, this yarn hasn't involved any spinning at all. However, you can take the process a step further and ply the rag "yarn" with another yarn before you knit with it. I have to admit I haven't done much with this technique, but I think it has exciting possibilities and deserves some experimentation.

How about cutting up an old silk dress, which happens to have a beautifully colored design, and plying it with one or

---

FEATHER YARNS. Sometimes one feather is caught at a time, sometimes two. Some feathers are wrapped through their full lengths, some just caught by the shaft.

two solid-colored silk yarns? The printed fabric would create the illusion of space dyeing.

The way to cut the fabric so you don't have to deal with a lot of short strips, is to cut it in spirals or back-and-forth, as shown in the diagrams. If you use the back-and-forth method, you will get a little bump at each end, where there will be extra fabric. You can cut fabric with the grain or on the bias. The closer you get to running on the bias, the stretchier your strips will be and the more their edges will ravel. The ravelling can add a nice texture, if you want it.

Ribbons can also be plied with yarns and then knitted or used in weaving.

Metallics

Shiny, shimmery, glittery **metallics** add a dressy look to a garment. I haven't yet figured how to create metallic yarns by spinning straw into gold. However, there are many ways to incorporate metallic yarns with handspuns by plying. They can be a bit scratchy, so sample for wearability if you plan to make a garment.

You can make a simple two-ply, using one strand of metallic and one of your base fiber. Use the metallic in a knot yarn, or as the binder in a bouclé.

Think about how glittery you want the finished yarn to be, and plan its proportions accordingly. Say you want a medium-weight yarn with just a glimpse of sparkle. Ply four fine yarns together (one metallic and three of other, related colors). You will have a yarn with 25 percent sparkle. Or ply a metallic with a fuzzy yarn, so you see mostly fluff with an occasional flash.

New horizons

For great fun and excitement after you have mastered the basics, try combining yarns which were spun with different techniques. Here are a few ideas to get your creative juices flowing.

- Loosely ply together one strand of fuzzy yarn, a fine bouclé, and a space-dyed commercial silk yarn. You can put them together all at once, or in sequence as in a crepe yarn.
- Spin a singles of multicolored silk noil, mohair, and silk top, all blended together. Make it into a bouclé, using a fine thread. Ply together two fine, space-dyed silk yarns — let one have all light values and one all dark values. Loosely ply together the bouclé and the space-dyed two-ply.

• Get your hands on a multicolored mercerized cotton: find some variegated crochet cotton, or space dye your own. Make a knot yarn which has different-colored knots. Then loosely ply it with a fuzzy yarn and a metallic.

• Make a three-ply crepe yarn. Of your three strands, use one that has beads strung on it and one that is of a different color. Ply the result loosely with a fine ribbon. Your imagination is the only limit.

Okay, now put it all together

BEADS, SEQUINS, AND METALLICS. The swatch was knitted from the bead yarn shown. The very fine metallic curling around it was one of the components in the blue two-ply, half-metallic yarn. ➡

Appendix

SUMMARY OF FIBER FORMS
AND DYEING RESULTS

Type of Fiber	Advantages / Disadvantages
Raw fiber	Fiber-dyed yarns can be fluffier than yarn-dyed ones. Yarn will not be streaky — you can blend out unevenness in carding. Yarn is finished as soon as it's spun. Best for heathered yarn and color blending. Fibers can felt in dyepot.
Prepared fiber — e.g., top or roving	If space-dyed, can give the effect of blending with less work. Necessary for color or fiber blending if your fiber comes in prepared form. Difficult to get dye to penetrate fully.
Yarn	Best for space-dyed yarn. Good if you want a more compact yarn, since dyeing may cause slight felting.

SUMMARY OF VARIEGATED-DYEING METHODS

	Advantages	Disadvantages
DIP DYEING	Controllable, repeatable	Regular, not random, time-consuming
DIRECT APPLICATION		
Spray	Covers large area	Wastes dye, is messy, doesn't dye center of fiber mass
Syringe	Good control, can produce lots of small areas of different colors	Slow, best for small quantities of fiber
Pouring	Quick, covers large area	Lack of control
Powder	Lots of small areas of color	Not repeatable; risk from airborne powder

Bibliography

Adams, Brucie. "Boiled Wool." *Handwoven* V:3 (Summer 1984): 85.

-----. "The Hair of the Dog." *Handwoven* III:2 (March 1982): 62-63.

-----. "Linsey-Woolsey Using Handspun Yarns." *Handwoven* III:5 (November/December 1982): 59-60.

-----. "Spinning for an Ombré Project." *Handwoven* IV:2 (March/April 1983): 78-79.

Amos, Alden. "Color Blending for the Spinner." *Spin·Off Quarterly Newsletter* (March 1982): 11-12.

-----. "Mercerizing: Not for Everyone." *Spin·Off* IX:2 (Summer 1985): 30.

Bartl, Pam. "Structuring a Bulky Yarn." *Interweave* V:2 (Spring 1980): 62-63. Discusses corespinning.

Benson, Sallyann. "Bulk Spinning." *Shuttle Spindle & Dyepot* XIV:issue 54 (Spring 1983): 36-38.

Birren, Faber. *The Textile Colorist.* New York: Van Nostrand Reinhold, 1980.

Bliss, Anne. "Blending Mohair with Other Fibers." *Spin·Off* VII:3 (Fall 1983): 43-44.

Bradley, Louise. "Ikat Spinning." *Handwoven* II:4 (September 1981): 65-67.

Burkhauser, Jude. "Handspun Yarn as Art." *Spin·Off Annual* vol. 3 (1979): 22.

Calhoun, Wheeler, and Lee Kirschner. "The Continuous Thread: From Flax Seed to Linen Cloth." *Spin·Off* VII:1 (Spring 1983): 28-31.

Chadwick, Eileen. *The Craft of Handspinning.* New York: Charles Scribner's Sons, 1980.

Chapin, Deloria. "Designer Yarns: Slubs and Spirals." *Spin·Off Annual* vol. 3 (1979): 54-55.

Chastant, Kathryn. "Angora Goats and Mohair." *Spin·Off* VII:3 (Fall 1983): 29-42.

Clark, Marlyn. "Twist Demystified." *Spin·Off* VII:2 (Summer 1983): 25-28.

-----. "Thick and Thin (and Lots in Between)." *Spin·Off Quarterly Newsletter* (March 1982): 4-5.

Davenport, Elsie. *Your Handspinning.* Tarzana, California: Select Books, 1964.

d'Avila, Doris. "Spinning Novelty Yarns." *Interweave* IV:4 (Fall 1979): 58-59.

-----. "Beyond the Machine (The Creative Use of Precision)." *Spin·Off Annual* vol 4 (1980): 50-52.

Deems, Flo. "Pointillist Color Effects in Spinning." *Spin·Off Annual* vol 4 (1980): 53-55.

Donohue, Sandra. "Spinning Unique and Useable Yarns." *Spin·Off* VIII:4 (Winter 1984): 33-34.

Fannin, Allen. *Handspinning: Art and Technique.* New York: Van Nostrand Reinhold, 1970.

Henrikson, Susan. " 'Union Dyes' and Another Look at a 'Rainbow' Pot." *Spin·Off* VI:4 (October 1982): 16-17.

Hochberg, Bette. "Add a New Twist to Your Spinning." *Spin·Off Annual* vol 5 (1981): 42-45.

Hodges, Susie, and Susan Druding. "Multi-colored Dyeing in One Pot." *Textile Artist's Newsletter* III:2 (1982).

Howard, Helen Griffiths. "The Musk Ox." *Spin·Off* VII:1 (Spring 1983): 16-19.

Howard, Miranda. "Angora: A Spinner's Delight." *Spin·Off* VI:4 (October 1982): 43-45.

Knutson, Linda. "Getting Started with Chemical Dyes." *Spin·Off* VIII:3 (Fall 1984): 39-41.

-----. *Synthetic Dyes for Natural Fibers.* Rev. ed. Loveland, Colorado: Interweave, 1986.

Leadbeater, Eliza. "Flax: Yarn Design Determines Choice." *Spin·Off* VIII:3 (Fall 1984): 34-35.

Leggett, Dawn. "Rx: Pills." *Spin·Off* VIII:4 (Winter 1984): 35-38.

Linder, Harry, and Olive Linder. *Handspinning Cotton.* Phoenix, Arizona: The Cotton Squares, 1977.

Linder, Olive. "Cotton: What Should You Ask For?" *Spin·Off* VIII:3 (Fall 1984): 36.

Lorance, Marilyn. "Rainbow Fleece." *Handwoven* II:4 (September 1981): 68-69.

Lynch, Mary Anne. "Rainbow Fleece: A Happy Hazard Approach to Chemical Dyeing." *Spin·Off Quarterly Newsletter* (December 1981): 8.

Metchette, Glenda. "Spinning Fancy Yarns." *Shuttle Spindle & Dyepot* XIV:issue 53 (Winter 1982): 16-19.

Milner, Ann. *I Can Spin a Different Thread.* New Zealand: J. McIndoe, 1981.

Murrow, Romedy. "Dealing with Dog Hair." *Spin·Off* VIII:1 (Spring 1984): 36-37.

Noble, Judy. "Designing Handspun." *Spin·Off Annual* vol 2 (1978): 53-55.

Omer, Martha. "Designer Yarn—A Use for Acid Dyes."
  Spin·Off VI:4 (October 1982): 56.

Quinn, Celia. "Elements of Yarn Structure." *Spin·Off* VI:4
  (October 1982): 46-51.

-----. "Fiber Foray: Spinning Combed Alpaca." *Spin·Off*
  IX:1 (Spring 1985): 26-27.

-----. "Ramie." *Spin·Off* VIII:4 (Winter 1984): 50-52.

-----. "Silk: A Fiber of Many Faces." *Spin·Off* VIII:3 (Fall
  1984): 30-33.

Raven, Lee. "Fiber Properties: Tenacity." *Spin·Off* VII:1
  (Spring 1983): 38.

Ross, Mabel. *The Essentials of Handspinning.* Kinross,
  Scotland: Mabel Ross, 1980.

-----. *The Essentials of Yarn Design for Handspinners.*
  Kinross, Scotland: Mabel Ross, 1983.

Rowe, Erica. "Angora: Frivolous Fluff or Fantastic Fiber?"
  Spin·Off VIII:2 (Summer 1984): 13-16.

Russell, Barbara. "Dyeing Mohair and the Random Effect."
  Spin·Off VI:4 (October 1982): 54-56.

Shapiro, Brenda. "Spray Dyeing to Obtain Space-Dyed
  Yarns." *Shuttle Spindle & Dyepot* XV:issue 60 (Fall 1984):
  54-56.

Stevens, Connie. "An Easy as Pie Dye Method." *Spin·Off*
  IX:1 (Spring 1985): 22-23.

Upitis, Lizbeth. "Fulled Knitting." *Knitters* III:1 (Fall/Winter
  1986): 34.

Walker, Linda Berry. "Handspinning as Art." *Spin·Off
  Annual* vol. 2 (1978): 56-58.

Wheeler, Barbara. "Wool: Mill-Prepared for Handspinners."
  Spin·Off VIII:3 (Fall 1984): 23-24.

Index